Euripides: Heracles

DUCKWORTH COMPANIONS
TO GREEK AND ROMAN TRAGEDY

Series editor: Thomas Harrison

Aeschylus: Agamemnon
Barbara Goward

Euripides: Heracles
Emma Griffiths

Euripides: Bacchae
Sophie Mills

Euripides: Hippolytus
Sophie Mills

Euripides: Medea
William Allan

Seneca: Phaedra
Roland Mayer

Seneca: Thyestes
P.J. Davis

Sophocles: Ajax
Jon Hesk

Sophocles: Electra
Michael Lloyd

Sophocles: Philoctetes
Hanna M. Roisman

Sophocles: Women of Trachis
Brad Levett

DUCKWORTH COMPANIONS
TO GREEK AND ROMAN TRAGEDY

Euripides: Heracles

Emma Griffiths

Duckworth

First published in 2006 by
Gerald Duckworth & Co. Ltd.
90-93 Cowcross Street, London EC1M 6BF
Tel: 020 7490 7300
Fax: 020 7490 0080
inquiries@duckworth-publishers.co.uk
www.ducknet.co.uk

A catalogue record for this book is available
from the British Library

ISBN 0 7156 3186 1

Printed and bound in Great Britain by
CPI Bath

Contents

Acknowledgements

I would like to thank Deborah Blake, Tom Harrison and the anonymous reader at Duckworth for their editorial input. My friends and colleagues at the University of Manchester have been a constant source of support. In keeping with Heracles' final words in this play, I dedicate this volume to Mary, Helen, Jane, Steve and Genevieve.

1

Introduction

Any man who wishes to have money or strength rather than good friends is out of his mind. (1425-6)

These closing words from Heracles as he leaves the stage at the end of the play refer to several key themes of the drama: the importance of friendship; the impotence of money or physical strength when faced with divine displeasure; and the importance of sanity. The final words, *kakôs phronei*, mean literally 'is thinking badly' or 'is mad', and the immediate point of reference is Heracles' own bout of 'bad thinking', the madness imposed by Hera, during which he killed his own wife and children. There seems to be a clear moral for an audience to draw from the play, but the events leading up to this final scene have not been so easy to interpret. The greatest hero of Greek mythology, a man depicted by Euripides as a devoted father, has lost it all because of divine jealousy. The play is shocking and leaves many questions unanswered.

To understand the full significance of this play as a reflection on cosmic reciprocity and the limits to mortal power we must understand the role of Heracles in the wider framework of Greek mythology. Starting from our own readings in the early twenty-first century we are confronted with a startling range of material to assimilate and bring to our appreciation of the play. The connection between a Disney cartoon and the founder of the Western Buddhist Order may not at first sight be obvious, but both have drawn artistic inspiration from the ancient figure of Heracles/Hercules, producing new works of drama and poetry which continue the development of the myth, now into its third millennium.[1] In the late twentieth and early twenty-first centuries Heracles may be the most well-known figure from Graeco-Roman mythology. As a man of many faces, he can be found in different cultures across the world, sometimes as the superhero, the strongman who completes the Labours, sometimes as an example of moral heroism, showing the ability to transcend human pain and become like a god. The responses of different individuals, historical periods and cultures have created a kaleidoscope of images which may be brought to mind when we hear the name Heracles today, and yet the ancient figure was equally complex – there is no one simple original. From the earliest images we can find in Greek culture Heracles was the subject of stories which highlighted different, often conflicting, accounts of his behaviour and character. The myth of Heracles can be schematised into a rough biographical structure, ranging from his birth as son of Zeus, through his completion of the Labours, to his death and deification, but such a schematic account would fail to account for the changes of mood, attitude and action which make up this most puzzling, yet compelling, mythological hero.

Although Euripides' *Heracles* has not traditionally been seen as one of Greek Tragedy's Greatest Hits, it has received greater attention in recent years both from academic critics, who have explored the play as a quintessentially Euripidean challenge, and from the theatrical community, who have staged a number of productions. The survival of the play itself for more than nearly 2,500 years owes as much to chance as to any perennial value placed on it as a work of literature. The examples of Greek tragedy we can read today are only a fraction of the hundreds of plays which were produced in the heyday of fifth-century Athens, and the few which survive come to us by different routes. By the Byzantine era only twenty-three plays had been chosen for preservation, and *Heracles* was not among them.[2] We have this play because of the chance preservation of another line of manuscripts which contained several other Euripidean plays. Put in crudest terms, the play survives because its title in Greek begins with an 'E' (*Erakles Mainomenos – Mad Heracles*), a point we will return to in the final chapter when we consider the transmission and reception history. Scholars have at times subjected the play to harsh criticism, with particular opprobrium directed towards the play's episodic structure. However, the play does contain themes and ideas which are fundamental to many of the more popular tragedies. The difficulties of interpretation which this play poses have been seen by recent critics as a mark of Euripides' genius, a challenge to the audience, rather than an indication of dramaturgical incompetence. As an instantiation of one part of the myth it was part of the wider process of mythological and historical thinking current in fifth-century Athens. As a piece of drama it challenges audiences ancient and modern to confront the very nature of illusion and storytelling.

In this volume we will be primarily examining the play within its original context, exploring the ways it related to issues and ideas current when it was originally produced some time in the late fifth century. Chapters 2 and 3 will outline the mythological background which the original audience would have brought to the play and indicate the mythological significance of the story, then proceed to examine the literary tradition in which the play was created. Chapter 4 will examine the structure of the play as a piece of theatre, with particular attention to issues of staging. The following four chapters will focus on key aspects of the drama; and Chapter 9 will consider the reception of the play and its role in present day society. Although the chapters are designed to be read in sequence, developing ideas from one theme to another, there is some repetition of key points together with cross-referencing, for those who may be interested in a particular aspect of the play.

Tragedy and the 'universal'

Before we turn to Heracles himself, a word of caution is in order. Greek tragedy still finds audiences some 2,500 years after it was written and first performed. There is a tension between understanding the play in its original Greek setting and appreciating our own reactions. Are we responding to new things in the play, or are we responding to the same things because of shared instincts? Is our basic ability to respond to the same material, to return to issues of society and individual, an indication of some constant, some universality in the plays? The key idea, that human nature remains constant and that Greek myths speak to that core humanity, can be formulated in many ways. We can look to the psychoanalytical idea expressed by Jung that there are archetypes in the collective unconscious: Jung believed that we all inherited a mental set of patterns which we use to create our own place in the world, assigning to ourselves and others a role from a limited number of 'archetypes'. The mental pattern book was the same across different cultures and periods of history, which is why, Jung believed, we are able to relate to ancient cultures as to our own. Such ideas were taken up by Joseph Campbell, whose writings on mythology influenced George Lucas when he created the modern 'myth' of the Star Wars films. A related approach is the anthropological stance associated particularly with Lang, which argues that all human cultures progress via the same stages, so that similar motifs develop independently.[3] When we look at a Greek tragedy it is easy to apply these stories to our own lives, ignoring the details and focusing on emotions or fundamental human concerns, such as family or love. However, this line of argument can be deceptive.

The principle of universality belongs to a set of ideas from a particular period of history, when the idea of universality across periods and cultures was popular in many fields.[4] Many of the central ideas have been challenged by later intellectual developments. We will be looking at a number of approaches which could be termed 'universalising' as we proceed through the discussions, but it is as well to note some of the principal objections which could be raised.

The opposing view to universal theories comes from the idea of cultural and social constructs. Instead of positing a universal human nature, the idea of constructs emphasises the degrees of interaction between individuals and groups which can create new patterns of meaning. So, on a simple level, the act of nodding the head forward in Britain means 'yes', whereas in Greece it means 'no'.[5] This principle can be taken further. Some have argued that even things which we might assume to be universal, such as the experience of the physical body, are subject to a process of cultural mediation. We may all experience the same biological phenomena, but the ways in which we understand and deal with the process are determined by society. So, for example, women's bodies have often been treated as inherently imperfect – the Hippocratic approach to women is well discussed by King and can be seen even today in the loaded term 'hysteria', a madness associated with having a uterus.[6]

Does Heracles become hysterical in Euripides' play? How does this affect our view of his sexual and gendered identity?[7] In the final chapter we will explore how recent decades have linked the story of Heracles' madness to the story of Medea, and found striking differences in the way ancient and modern audiences contemplated filicide in relation to the construction of gender.

The idea of constructs warns us to be wary when we think we can transfer ideas or images from one culture to another. A striking example of this approach to mythology comes from Freud's use of the Oedipus myth. The famous play by Sophocles was, for its original fifth-century Greek audience, not a play about psychological trauma, but one about the inevitability of fate. A story can have different meanings in two different contexts.[8] The story of a man who kills his children can be variously interpreted, depending on how a society understands the idea of 'man', 'killing', 'children' etc. In the ancient world the story may be about man's relationship with the gods, the obligations of reciprocity between man and god, and between friends. In the modern world the same play can speak to audiences about the social construction of masculinity and the role of violence in society. Standing between these two ends is a long process of change and reinterpretation through different cultures and times. Heracles in the ancient world and in the modern presents a bewildering range of images. There is a tendency to impose our own order on the mass of images, and to make a coherent picture based on our own beliefs and assumptions.

The main focus of this volume will be the *ancient* role of the play. Nevertheless, some would argue that it is impossible for us to look back at the play as it was in its original production, because we are unavoidably conditioned by all the later images which stand between us and the ancient sources. There are two schools of thought implicated in this issue. The one, persuasively articulated by Sourvinou-Inwood, argues that we can develop an understanding of the original ancient world if we collect enough information to construct 'perceptual filters'.[9] By applying these 'filters', as if putting on a pair of glasses, we can look back into the ancient world. This approach, sometimes referred to as working with a 'cultural encyclopaedia', is central to much of the work traditionally undertaken in the field of classical studies. The opposing view, from a more recent, post-structuralist perspective, argues that it is impossible to escape our own mental framework. This view, proposed by Martindale and others, favours an approach which emphasises the reception history of the ancient world.[10] By gaining a greater awareness of the distance which stands between us and the ancient world we become more self-conscious about our own roles in creating history. Viewed from such a perspective, ancient mythology is not something fixed which influences later cultures. Rather, there is a dynamic process of interaction between the two, whereby modern ideas and constructs affect our ability to access the ancient world and thus change the ancient mythology. This volume aims to provide material for those wishing to approach the play from either perspective, and to encourage the development of independent assessment. To that end, the discussions will not advance one single reading of the play, but will indicate different approaches and suggest reasons for the most popular readings in current critical thinking.

2

Heracles and Greek Myth

The *mythos* is not single by virtue of having only a single hero ...
The authors of the Lives of Heracles seem to be mistaken ...
insofar as they believe that, simply because there is only one
hero, there is necessarily unity in the story.

Aristotle, *Poetics* 1451a16 ff.

This quotation from the early fourth century indicates that
ancient writers and audiences faced similar problems to those we
confront today when trying to comprehend the figure of
Heracles. A desire to impose structure must contend with the
multiplicity of stories told about Heracles which cannot be simply
reconciled into one coherent biography, but for the sake of con-
venience a brief overview of the major episodes is offered here.

Mythic biography[1]

Heracles' story is complicated from the circumstances of his
conception. Our earliest sources call him the child of Zeus and
a mortal mother, Alcmene, but in some versions Zeus had
appeared disguised as Alcmene's husband Amphitryon: the first
explicit account of this disguise comes in Pindar *Nemean* 10.13-
18. Alcmene is also said to have conceived a second son by
Amphitryon on the same night, so that Heracles' 'twin' brother,
Iphicles, is in fact his half-brother. This overlap of parentage is
an important element of the family dynamic in Euripides' play.
As a child, Heracles' superhuman strength was apparent when
he strangled the snakes which attacked him in his cradle, an
early attack by Hera.[2] On reaching adulthood, Heracles was
involved in a number of stories in locations across the known

world, such as the first destruction of the walls of Troy, or the killing of the Egyptian King Busiris. The most famous of his miraculous feats of strength formed a sequence of events conventionally termed 'The Labours'.

At various stages of his career Heracles fathered a number of children. Many Greek communities claimed to be his direct descendants, particularly in the Dorian communities of the Peloponnese: Herodotus described how the authority of the Spartan ephors was related to their claim to trace descent from Heracles (Herodotus, *Histories* 5.39-42).[3] Heracles had two wives, but neither marriage ended well. Megara was killed by Heracles (as Euripides tells us), and Deianeira killed herself after inadvertently causing Heracles' death (the events of Sophocles' *Women of Trachis*). At the end of his life, the gods rewarded Heracles by making him divine, and marrying him to Hebe, goddess of youth. After his death, Heracles retained an interest in the affairs of mortals and was worshipped across Greece in the classical period both as a hero (semi-divine) and as a god, a double status unique in Greek cult.

Origins and the study of myth

Many mythological figures are known mainly for one single episode or a series of episodes, but Heracles' life was a source of incident from his birth through to his death and deification. He played a role in many other important strands of myth, with links to other mythological figures, and he had local associations across the Greek world. It is quite likely that many stories attached to the figure of Heracles were originally told of other mythological figures. Herodotus (2.41-3) suggested that Heracles was of Egyptian descent, a claim strongly denied by Plutarch, who asserts that the earliest Greeks (in his terms, Homer and Hesiod) knew only of an Argive, or a Boeotian, Heracles.[4] Pausanias (9.27.8) suggests that there was also a less famous Heracles, one of the Dactyls of Ida (the first metallurgists associated with the worship of Cybele).

Many theories have been proposed for the original or central ideas which comprise the 'Myth of Heracles'. This is not a new preoccupation, as Herodotus noted the similarities between Heracles and divinities in other cultures, particularly those associated with the Sun (2.45). Some modern approaches have focused on Heracles' actions as a fertility symbol: Jourdain-Annequin draws attention to the killing of Geryon as the 'triple monster, image of death', and suggests that Heracles was a fertility figure who overcame chthonic powers.[5] The defeat of monsters can also be seen as a representation of mankind's ability to tame nature through cultivation, with Heracles as the civilising, socialising figure. Dumézil suggested that Heracles was an example of the Indo-European type 'Hero-Warrior', comparing him with Tullus Hostilius and Horatius in Roman myth, and Indra and Trita Aptypa in Indian myth.[6] For Dumézil, the characters are linked because each initially fulfils a role useful to society, protecting his family from an enemy, but then the violence spills over and the hero kills members of his own family. Heracles' stories have been viewed in terms of folk-tale patterns as tales of the Strong Man, or the Quest figure.[7] Others have viewed him as a liminal figure who represents a struggle between life and death (on structuralist readings). He is also an ideal subject for post-structuralist analysis as an inherently ambiguous figure, something between life and death, mortal and immortal, or even between male and female as Loraux has demonstrated.[8] Heracles is often associated with the crossing of boundaries and, therefore, initiation myths, but Pralon has argued persuasively that the version of the Labours given in Euripides' *Heracles* does not use this stratum of myth, as Heracles is shown as an adult and father.[9] A full account of the debates surrounding the origins or central meaning of Heracles' myths falls outside the scope of this volume, and the value of such debates is highly contested. Reductionist readings of myth which attempt to explain complex phenomena in terms of simple ones are often attractive, but run the risk of eliding material which is not easily fitted to a schematic account. Further information for those who wish to explore the myths of Heracles can be found in the section on further reading, but the following discussions will focus on ideas which are relevant to the study of the Madness of Heracles.

Heracles in Homer

Heracles has a strong mythological persona in the earliest surviving literary works of the eighth century BCE, and the wealth of detail suggests that the stories were well known much earlier. The two narrative poems, the *Iliad* and *Odyssey*, took shape some time in the eighth century BCE, but derived from a far older tradition of songs, composed and sung without the aid of writing.[10] In the *Iliad*, the story of one period during the Greek siege of Troy, Heracles is mentioned a number of times, in contexts which stress his close connection to issues of mortality. The capture of Cerberus is the only Labour mentioned specifically, an act which symbolises a triumph over death, and hence mortality. The circumstances of his conception and birth are mentioned by Zeus himself (*Iliad* 14.323-4) and by Agamemnon (*Iliad* 19.95-125). Heracles' death is referred to by Achilles, who reflects on his own mortality, the fact that he will die despite having an immortal parent:

> ... As for my own fate,
> I'll accept it whenever it pleases Zeus
> And the other immortal gods to send it.
> Not even Heracles could escape his doom.
> He was dearest of all to Lord Zeus, but fate
> And Hera's hard anger destroyed him.
>
> *Iliad* 18.122-8[11]

The implication of this comparison is that Heracles, like Achilles, was mortal and died a mortal death, i.e. he was not deified as later traditions told. The *Odyssey* presents a different version of the story when Odysseus, sailing home from Troy, summons figures from Hades and encounters not Heracles' ghost, but rather some representation of Heracles:

> And then mighty Heracles loomed up before me –
> His phantom that is, for Heracles himself
> Feasts with the gods and has as his wife
> Beautiful Hebe, daughter of great Zeus
> And gold-sandalled Hera. As he moved

2. Heracles and Greek Myth

A clamor arose from the dead around him,
As if they were birds flying off in terror.
Odyssey 11.630-6[12]

Here we seem to have a version of the story in which Heracles does not die as a mortal, but is taken to Olympus.[13] As the *Iliad* and *Odyssey* were composed at a similar time in similar circumstances, some scholars have argued that the reference to 'Heracles' phantom' in the *Odyssey* cannot be original, and must have been added by later generations for whom the deification of Heracles was a standard part of the story. Kirk, however, has suggested that the contradictions of Heracles' story were part of the original strata of myth, so that our confusion may be part of the process.[14] A similar process of confusion can be seen in the image of Heracles as 'dearest to Zeus' (*Iliad* 18.115-21), but also as a 'godless man attacking the gods' (*Iliad* 5.403-4). Heracles' multivalency and his liminal status will prove to be central ideas in Euripides' play.

The Labours and the Madness

In Euripides' *Heracles*, the chorus of old men sing of the Labours of Heracles (348ff.), outlining twelve separate feats of bravery: the Nemean Lion; the Killing of the Centaurs; the Hind; the Thracian Mares; Kyknos; the Hesperides; the Sea-clearing; Atlas; the Amazons; the Hydra; Geryon; Hades. This set of twelve is not co-extensive with the set of twelve found on the Temple of Zeus at Olympia (the Centaurs, the Hesperides, Kyknos and the Sea-clearing are given in place of the alternative Labours, the Boar, the Birds, the Augean Stables and the Cretan Bull, found at Olympia). As Bond notes, the Euripidean version is Panhellenic and emphasises Heracles' role as saviour of mankind.[15] We should also note that the Labours were illustrated on the Athenian Hephaesteum (referred to in older scholarship as the Theseum).[16] The general outline of the story is that Heracles was forced to serve the king Eurystheus, and was set by him a number of seemingly impossible tasks such as killing the Lernaean Hydra, a monster with several heads, or

19

cleaning the huge Augean stables. Heracles accomplished his tasks with a mixture of unnatural strength and cunning: in the case of the Hydra, he prevented each severed head from turning into two new ones by cauterising each stump, and he cleaned the Augean stables by diverting a river through them.

The Labours are a central feature of Heracles' story, as there are references to his 'trials', *aethloi*, in Homer (*Iliad* 8.363, *Odyssey* 11.622).[17] However, there is no canonical chronology, and the relationship between the Labours, the Madness and the death of Heracles' children can be variously configured. Euripides explains the Labours as Heracles' attempt to restore his family home to Argos/Tiryns, placing the murder of the children *after* the achievement of the final Labour, the removal of Cerberus from Hades. Euripides' version is the earliest surviving account to make a chronology explicit, but there are reasons to suspect that this is his own invention. Pre-Euripidean sources give us only scattered and conflicting pieces of information about the death of the children. The marriage to Megara appears in our earliest literary sources, as does mention of Heracles' madness. The first specific references to a frenzied *infanticide* by Heracles come from the sixth/fifth century BCE authors Stesichorus and Panyasis. While the works of these writers survive only in fragments, Pausanias, writing in the second century CE, summarises their accounts and implies that Heracles committed the murders while mad.[18] Pherecydes, from the sixth century BCE, tells how Heracles threw his five children into a fire, a version which accords with the earliest surviving artistic representation of the episode (discussed in Chapter 9). This version has mythological resonance, as fire and the loss of immortality are linked motifs, according to structuralist analysis of myth.[19] Pindar (*Isthmian* 4.61-4) mentions a sacrifice made to the eight children of Heracles, but his account may suggest that the sons died as adults, for they are described as 'fitted with bronze', which may mean 'armed'.

For a clear account of the place of the infanticide within the life history of Heracles we must look to later writers. Apollodorus, writing in the second century BCE, gives the events as Madness followed by Labours, possibly with the Labours as a penance for the murders.[20] While this account comes from a source written many generations after Euripides' play, there are several reasons to suspect that this is a pre-Euripidean version, as Wilamowitz argued.[21] Firstly, Apollodorus often appears to gather his information from a range of early, and sometimes pre-fifth-century, sources. It is also the case that the form of myths told in tragedy often came to dominate later accounts, obscuring earlier versions, rather than being obscured themselves by later versions. A further argument suggesting that the standard model was Madness followed by Labours is that the general mythological pattern of cause and effect is much stronger if the Labours are a punishment for a terrible act. This would correspond to another strand of Heracles' story, as his enslavement to Omphale is punishment for another violent act, the murder of Iphitus, son of Eurytus of Oechalia. The *scholia* to Pindar *Isthmian* 4.1045 says that Heracles was mad when he killed Iphitus.

The sequence of events given in Euripides' play has great dramatic potential, suggesting a more conscious process of construction. It allows Euripides to place Heracles firmly within a family context, and points up the contrast between domestic affairs and actions of global significance. When Heracles recovers from the Madness there is a gaping hole in his life story, which can only be filled by human resources. Euripides' hero cannot atone for this crime by undertaking superhuman tasks, he can only turn to friends for support.

Images of Heracles

We may categorise Heracles as a man of extremes, for good or ill, and in Euripides' play the hero is often described with superlatives, 'best of friends', 'most wretched of men' etc. He is also a figure of contradictions, the violent warrior who expresses a desire to care for his children. Although this particular image of Heracles is useful for Euripides' dramatic purposes, there are contradictions already inherent in the myth. Heracles is at times shown as the drunk, the glutton and the lecher, but he can also be held up as a moral exemplar. His role as cult figure, worshipped both as a hero and as a god, provides a further source of associations, and raises questions about the relationship between religion and the myths as told in artistic sources. This chapter will conclude by turning to the socio-historical implications of his mythology, with discussion of the term 'hero' and its place within fifth-century Athenian democracy.

Heracles the man of passions

The degree of force which Heracles displays in killing his children can be seen as part of a pattern of violent actions. In Chapter 6 we will discuss one of the central problems of the play, whether Heracles' actions are out of character or merely misdirected, but in general Heracles was often portrayed as a man of excessive passions. He is involved in the drunken fight between the Centaurs and the Lapiths,[22] and his appetite for food and drink is referred to in numerous places, including Euripides' play *Alcestis*, where Heracles is initially portrayed as a loud, boisterous guest. Self-control was highly valued among most ancient Greek societies, and most heroes in myth undergo some form of training or education aimed at promoting restraint and balance.[23] It is a notable feature of Heracles' story that he received only limited guidance. As a youth he killed his teacher Linus and was, therefore, sent into the countryside until he came of age.[24] Passion, be it for food, drink or sex, is a dominant feature of his life story.

These passions can at times interfere with his missions. Heracles was one of the original crew who sailed with Jason in the Argo to capture the Golden Fleece, but he failed to complete the journey. He was led astray by his passion for one of his young companions – Hylas was captured by nymphs and Heracles abandoned his mission to search for him:

(On hearing of Hylas' loss)
When Herakles heard this, sweat poured down over his temples
    and deep in his body
the dark blood boiled. In a rage he threw the fir-tree to the
    ground and ran wildly

22

> wherever his feet led him. As when a bull is stung by a gadfly
>   and rushes off,
> abandoning the meadows and the marshes, and has no thought
>   for the keepers or the
> herd, but runs without resting, or sometimes stops to bellow in
>   distress at the bite of
> the cruel fly, so in his rage did Herakles' legs move swiftly ...[25]

His sexual passions are also harmful to his family in the story told in Sophocles' *Women of Trachis*. Some time after his marriage to Megara and the death of the children, Heracles married Deianeira. After killing Iphitus and serving his time as slave to Omphale, Heracles waged war on Oechalia in order to take princess Iole as a concubine. When he returned home, his wife Deianeira was so distressed by the situation that she attempted to win back Heracles' love with a charm, which subsequently led to his death.

The idea of the man of extreme passions will form the basis of the comic Heracles discussed in the next chapter, but there is something disturbing about the violence and lack of restraint shown by Heracles, more suited to tragic treatments. Heracles shows little respect for the usual social or personal boundaries which operated in Greek society, and this provides a parallel to the broader existential liminality created by the circumstances of his birth.

The philosophical hero

It is a paradox within the myth that the persona of 'violent, gluttonous, drunk' co-exists with the image of Heracles the saviour and moral hero. The Labours have a significance outside their immediate context, as they are often presented as acts which benefit all mankind. Heracles' actions are presented as those of the noble saviour, making the world a better place. His deification is a mark of his worth, and the motif of Heracles the saviour is important to Euripides' play, as he arrives to save the family from Lycus.

The idea of Heracles as a role model is linked to his portrayal as a man of great moral strength. His worldly success is attributed not to brute force, but to powers of endurance and moral strength of character. The ethical hero is the model of Heracles given in Pindar, *Nemean* 1.63, *Olympian* 10.34 and *Olympian* 9.30ff.[26] It is also the basis of the famous story told by the sophist Prodicus about how Heracles as a young man was forced to choose between a comfortable life of vice or a hard but honourable life of virtue, as told by Xenophon (*Memorabilia* 2.1.21-34). Kuntz's analysis of the story concludes that Prodicus may have created the story himself, on the model of the Judgement of Paris, but the story fitted well with Heracles' persona as saviour of mankind, and remained a popular part of the myth throughout the Western world.[27] The fact that he chose virtue and service to mankind connects him with his role after his death, interceding to help mortals who pray for his help. Similarly, his power to conquer death, as symbolised in the capture of Cerberus or the golden apples of the Hesperides, can be seen as a gift to all humanity, although, as we will see in later chapters, this power carries with it inherent dangers.

In Euripides' play, the hero's struggle with the idea of the gods, what might today be termed a 'crisis of faith', provides a window into Heracles' character as moral exemplar, and Theseus calls him 'the one who has endured all things' (1250). From this Greek model it was only a small step to the Hercules of Roman myth who became the Stoic examplar of virtue.

Heracles the cult figure

So far we have looked at Heracles as a figure of myth as seen in various literary and artistic sources, but his role in Greek cult introduces other issues. Heracles was a peculiar figure in Greek religion, worshipped both as a 'hero', i.e. a semi-divine former mortal (son of Amphitryon or Zeus), and as a god (deified son of Zeus). Pindar, *Nemean* 3.22, describes him as a 'hero god', but Verbanck-Piérard has argued that the double worship of hero/god was not a widespread phenomenon, and that the majority of cults were of the divine Heracles.[28] The origins of his cult are obscure, but from the sixth century BCE onwards his worship proliferated rapidly across the Greek world. He was adopted by many different groups within Greek society, and was often used as a symbol of social inclusion, through his image as a god of feasting.

In Athens, young men dedicated a lock of hair to him when they reached manhood, as part of the ritual of initiation, the symbolic crossing of the boundary between childhood and adulthood, and Heracles was associated with similar 'coming of age' ceremonies in many Greek states, as Jourdain-Annequin has demonstrated.[29] Heracles was also linked to initiation into the Eleusinian mysteries, as he is in Euripides' play. He tells Amphitryon that his success in capturing Cerberus was due to (or possibly just 'after') he 'saw the mysteries' (613), and Lloyd Jones has argued that there was a stronger tradition of accounts of this *katabasis*, a ritual descent, than we realise from our existing sources.[30] Heracles is frequently positioned in a nexus of ideas about immortality and resurrection: Mathieu notes that there is not a straight opposition between mortality and immortality, because figures often have to go through death to achieve immortality.[31] The Athenian context and the Eleusinian mysteries also had political associations, for Peisistratus, the Athenian tyrant, established many ritual practices, and encouraged identification with the figure of Heracles.[32] We should also note in connection with the play *Heracles* that Winkler has argued for a strong connection between drama and the role of ephebes in Athens.[33]

Heroism and democracy

In religious terms Heracles has an anomalous position as both 'hero' and 'god', but in popular culture he can be viewed as a 'hero' in terms closer to the modern use of the word. In the twenty-first century Euripides' *Heracles* may be most intelligible as an exploration of 'what it means to be a hero', i.e. as a dramatisation of the varying demands placed on an outstanding individual struggling with divided loyalties to his family and to wider responsibilities. Can the violent strength and dedication needed for superhuman endeavours allow an individual to experience the pleasures of an 'ordinary life'? This is the question posed by Simon Armitage in his reworking of the play as *Mister Heracles*. In the introduction to the play he spells out his interpretative stance:

> What do we mean by hero? What is the greatest atrocity a man can commit? Who can apportion blame to the workings of the human mind, and who has the power to forgive? These are the questions that face any reworking of the Heracles fable.[34]

The explosion of violence within the household of Heracles has been compared by some to cases of war veterans who commit acts of violence against their families;[35] the experience of military violence is said to cause deep-seated psychological trauma, such that the impulse towards violence necessary in one context becomes transferred to situations where it is highly inappropriate.[36] Bowman has argued that the play is related to attempts to reintegrate Athenian war veterans back into society.[37] In later chapters we will explore the possibility that Heracles' maddened actions are in some sense connected to his role as a violent fighter, but we must first establish what we mean by the word 'hero' outside the Greek ritual context.

Modern heroes come in many guises. There are those who perform jobs which take courage, strength or unusual talents (fire-fighters, football players, successful actors); there are those who struggle cheerfully to live life to the full despite physical or mental illness or difficult circumstances; there are those whose actions go beyond our normal expectations, the men and women who save children from burning houses or walk hundreds of miles to raise money for charity and so on. What all these heroes have in common is that they all represent a triumph of *human* ability. The original Greek word 'hero' (*hêrôs*), however, refers to a figure with a semi-divine status, the cult figure discussed above. Modern terminology has elevated man to this semi-divine status, so that figures who today possess superhuman abilities, such as the heroes of comic books and movies, have to move up a rung linguistically to become 'Superheroes'.[38] This is not the place to discuss the progress of this apparent humanisation of vocabulary, nor to discuss the difference between an hero and a heroine, so it must suffice to note that our current English conception of the hero prioritises human experience. When we say that we identify with a hero's struggles today, we may not imply that we imagine ourselves to be on a par with the hero, only that we see in their experience something which we can apply to our own situation.

To identify with a hero in the strictest Greek sense of the word would be to draw parallels between our mortal experience and that of a divine figure, a more problematic process of identification. If we leave precise terminology to one side, we may, however, ask whether the fifth-century Athenians had any concept closer to our idea of 'the hero', either as a mortal who achieves great things, or as a central figure within a narrative. The answer to this question is 'Yes', but with some reservations. Mortals could be honoured and respected for military or sporting success, but there persisted a religious scruple that such praise should be limited. It was widely believed that to be outstanding could be dangerous. For an individual to be so special that they were like a god would be an act of *hybris*, an offence of pride against the gods, which would be punished by divine retribution, an act of *nemesis*.[39] Such religious approaches were common throughout Greece, but the political situation in fifth-century Athens provided a very particular context for individual heroism.

Heroism in Athens

By the time that Euripides produced *Heracles* Athens had been run as a radical democracy for several generations.[40] All Athenian citizens, i.e. men who had Athenian fathers and mothers, were involved in political life, voting on public business in the assembly, known as the *ekklêsia*. Apart from the military office of General, all political officials were elected by lot, which gave even the poorest citizens the chance of direct involvement in city affairs. This form of government encouraged an egalitarian view of the individual's role in the community which placed limits on what was acceptable in terms of heroic action.

The heroes of the Homeric epics were strong characters who acted for individual glory as much as for the collective good, but in democratic Athens the individual's role was seen very much in terms of contribution to the good of the city. In a speech delivered to mark the funeral of the war dead in 431 BCE, the general Pericles is reported to have downplayed the role of individual endeavour in favour of greater attention to the wider interests of the state.[41] In the fifth century, warfare was no longer a matter of great strong men fighting individual battles, but of large collections of men working as units, allowing little room for spontaneous heroism.[42]

This arrangement affected peace-time activities as well. While the democratic system distributed most positions of power at random, there remained real possibilities for unofficial power, especially for those who were clever public speakers. The ability to persuade an audience to vote in a certain way was a skill that was taught to wealthy young men in Athens by a group of travelling teachers known as the sophists. Such unofficial routes to power and influence did not go unnoticed, and while the general population was often swayed by the political skills of one or other speaker, the city had a way of preventing any one man from gaining too much power in the democracy. From around 487 BCE the city had the political tool of *ostracism*, a vote taken by the citizen body to remove any individual from the city for period of time.[43] Athens had been ruled by a series of powerful individuals, tyrants, for many years in the sixth century, and the fear of such a situation remained alive throughout the fifth century. Therefore, in political terms, the idea of the great individual striking out on his own, taking heroic action, did not sit easily with Athenian democratic principles.

In terms of literature, the figure of the hero was again open to interpretation. Easterling has argued that the audiences of fifth-century tragedy were able to identify with the situations faced by a tragic character, putting aside differences of class, historical period or mortality, so that the heroes of drama were literary figures who could represent different ideas for an audience.[44] Certainly the Homeric epics retained an important place in Greek culture even when the individual heroic model which they promoted was not directly relevant to later Greek societies. As we will discuss further in the next chapter, tragedy presented its original audience with stories set in a mythical past whose customs and values were not identical to those of contemporary society. Those stories were, nonetheless, considered worthy of the effort to reshape and rework them for new times. The level of debate in tragedy indicates the presence of a wider community which was sophisticated in its understanding of myth and literature. The audience members, or at least some of them, were able to appreciate a dramatic figure on several levels, from absolute belief to complex philosophical and allegorical symbolism. Thus, having begun this section by emphasising the differences between modern and ancient ideas of the hero, we seem to close with a similarity in the idea of the hero as the focus of a narrative. We should, nonetheless, be constantly aware in studying the play that for the original audience there was a complex religious, as well as literary, background to the drama.

Conclusions

Some or all of the ideas discussed above were available to the original audience of Euripides' play, but beyond that it is difficult to assess the mindsets of members of the fifth-century audience, or of the playwright himself. Rather than pursue the detail of what may or may not be relevant background material, we should perhaps focus more on the process, noting that the fluidity of myth is part of its appeal, and that the myth of Heracles is particularly fertile.

What is missing from this survey of the myth is any clear parallel for the picture of Heracles as devoted family man which is fundamental to Euripides' play. The background for such a reading of the myth comes from the traditions of drama in Athens, so the following chapter will focus on the Athenian theatre, the traditions of Heracles as a dramatic character in tragedy and comedy, and the particular role of Euripides.

3

Euripides, Heracles and Greek Tragedy

Athenian drama in context

By the time Euripides was born some time in the late 480s BCE, tragedy was a well-developed genre as part of Athens' annual festival of the City Dionysia, a celebration of the god Dionysus, involving sacrifices, processions and competitions. Every year city officials chose three competitors who were each provided with financial backing to stage three tragedies and a satyr play apiece. The plays were performed in the Theatre of Dionysus, an outdoor space in the centre of Athens, which had become formalised as a theatre with some stone buildings and seats by the late fifth century. The physical staging can be described briefly as follows. The spectators, up to 16,000, were seated on the slopes of the Acropolis in a rough semi-circle. In the earliest period temporary wooden benches were erected, but as the fifth century progressed stone seats were introduced. The acting area below was roughly divided into two areas. The front area was called the *orchêstra*, 'dancing space', roughly twenty metres in diameter, with an altar in the centre. Further back was the area for the actors, where there may have been a slightly raised platform, but certainly not what we today would think of as a stage. During the early fifth century stage buildings were simple wooden constructions with doors for exits and entrances.

As the century progressed, permanent stone buildings were erected to act as scene/backstage areas. These backdrops provided basic scenery for the plays with the addition of some extra material such as painted screens. There were also a number of additional possibilities which were introduced at some point during the fifth century. Actors could appear on top of the stage buildings, through a trapdoor in the stage area, on a crane, the *mêchanê*, or on a wheeled extra stage, the *ekkyklêma*, which could be used to bring indoor scenes into the main acting space. The acting roles were divided among three male actors, who would usually play a number of parts in each play, supported by a small number of non-speaking actors. The *orchêstra* was reserved for the chorus, made up of twelve or fifteen men who sang and danced with the accompaniment of a flute- or *aulos*-player. The entire play was written in verse using a poetic style of language, somewhat different from everyday speech. All actors and chorus members were male, and wore simple wicker masks to assume the identity of the characters. Dionysus, the god of theatre, was also the god of masks, and in a wider sense the god of all transformations. Theatre was physically situated in the heart of Athens, under the Acropolis where the great temples were constructed, on a slope which afforded a good view over the city.[1]

Drama and the *polis*

All these festivals fall nominally under the aegis of the gods, and nearly all involve some obvious appurtenances of what could be called religion (sacrifice, prayer, temple or sacred site ceremonial), the separation of 'religion' as a discrete aspect of polis life is quite misleading.

Goldhill, 'Programme Notes', p. 20

The institution of drama within the religious festival was central to Athenian life, not a separate artistic endeavour. It was funded by the state, through a tax on the wealthy citizens called a liturgy. Each of the three chosen competitors was responsible for writing and producing his own set of plays, and prizes were awarded for the best playwright/director (*didaskalos*) and the best lead actor (the *protagonist*). The most significant prize for the playwright was the automatic right to compete in the following year's event. While fragments exist of plays by many fifth-century writers, entire plays have survived only from the works of Aeschylus, Sophocles and Euripides,

31

who were acknowledged in antiquity as the great tragedians of their time.

Euripides was the youngest of the three, being more than forty years younger than Aeschylus. To judge by the number of prizes he was the least successful, with only five known victories, but he achieved great popularity both during and after his lifetime: despite previous failures in the competition Euripides was regularly 'awarded a chorus', i.e. allowed to compete, in the next year's festival, and the survival of so many of his plays to the present day indicates the extent to which they were prized, and therefore copied, thus ensuring their transmission.[2] Today we have nineteen plays by Euripides, plus the *Cyclops*, a satyr play, and a tragedy, *Rhesus*, which may not have been written by Euripides.[3] For comparison, there are seven surviving works by Aeschylus, if we include *Prometheus Bound*, for which authorship is disputed.[4] Only seven plays of Sophocles have survived, which gives us a very small total out of the hundreds of tragedies presented in Athens during the fifth century alone.

The origins of tragedy as an art form are lost in the proverbial mists of time. It seems likely that the format grew out of the choral *dithyramb* competitions, and a single actor or narrator was added, an innovation sometimes attributed to the figure of Thespis, hence the English 'thespian'. As time went on another actor was added, introducing the possibility of dialogue and action, and this element gradually took precedence over the choral singing. In the classical period, three actors were allowed, but it is noticeable that Aeschylus makes very little use of the third actor, relying on one-to-one interactions to move the story along. Greek tragedy, as actions manifested rather than narrated, was still a new development at the start of the fifth century. Features such as the use of messenger speeches indicate how strongly the idea of dramatic narrative carried over into tragedy.[5] Undoubtedly Aeschylus was closer to the traditional origins of tragedy than were his younger colleagues. His style of language and characterisation was formal and closely allied to the traditions of epic poetry.[6] The younger playwright Sophocles produced a number of plays which focused on the personal crisis of a great heroic figure such as Oedipus or Ajax, often exploring the underlying characteristics of the great heroes known from epic poetry.[7] The small-scale medium of tragedy allowed playwrights to take existing stories and characters from myth and examine them from angles different from those adopted in epic poetry, so when Euripides came to write *Heracles*, he was part of a long literary tradition.

Heracles in tragedy

Heracles appears on stage as a character in four surviving tragedies, *Philoctetes* and *Women of Trachis* by Sophocles, and *Alcestis* and *Heracles* by Euripides. Each of the four surviving plays presents Heracles in a different light. In *Philoctetes* he appears as the deified hero to resolve the conflict between Philoctetes, Odysseus and Neoptolemus. He arrives with divine knowledge of the future, and is a model of diplomacy. Acting as a saviour, he resolves a conflict which for humans was insoluble, and functions as a mediator, playing a role comparable to that played by Theseus in other plays. Although he is personally linked to the story of Philoctetes via the bow, and he expresses a personal interest in the fall of Troy, his intervention comes as the 'deus ex machina' figure, an outside force devoid of any strong characteristics.[8] In *Alcestis* Heracles is again the saviour, helping his friend Admetus by rescuing his wife Alcestis from Hades and wrestling with Thanatos (Death).[9] Segal notes that in *Alcestis* Heracles is a good friend, and is sensitive towards Admetus' feelings.[10]

However, Heracles also appears in the play in his other role, as the party-animal. Before he realises that Alcestis has died he avails himself of Admetus' hospitality, causing the servant to comment disapprovingly on his heavy drinking (*Alcestis* vv. 747ff.). This Heracles is seen in Homer, as a violator of *xenia* (*Odyssey* 8.223-5, 21.11-41.), but it is a portrayal which is particularly close to the Heracles of comedy, and it is as well to note that *Alcestis* was presented by Euripides as a fourth play, i.e. in place of the traditional satyr play. Scholars are divided over the interpretation of the play, whether it should be viewed as a tragedy or a comedy.[11] It is possible to stage the play with a complete change in Heracles' persona once he realises the situation, and is horrified that he has been so insensitive to Admetus' grief. However, it is also plausible to see the play's close, with Heracles' teasing presentation of Alcestis, as a continuation of the hero's less serious role. We would then have a more intriguing situation where the roles of Heracles as drunken buffoon and saviour of mankind are seen as one and the same. This would complement other contradictions in the play, such as Admetus' wish to avoid his own death, and then his subsequent wish to die with Alcestis. Stevens notes that there is a distinct comic/colloquial feel to Heracles' language in the first episode of the play, but that his final speech is entirely heroic and formal.[12] We should also note that the motifs of *katabasis*, descent and return to Hades, link Alcestis and Heracles more broadly than through the actions of this one play alone.[13]

Women of Trachis and the lost plays

Sophocles' *Women of Trachis* has an immediate relevance for our appreciation of Euripides' *Heracles*, as it too shows Heracles' family context and the damage caused by his activities outside the domestic sphere.[14] The play opens as Heracles is returning from a campaign, bringing with him the captive Iole as his concubine. Heracles' wife, Deianeira, tries to win back Heracles' affection with a love charm, which turns out to be poisoned. The drama ends when the hero is brought on stage dying, and gives instructions to his son, Hyllus, to take care of his funeral and to marry Iole.

Sophocles' treatment of the story differs in emphasis from Euripides' play in a number of ways. Firstly, the agent of Heracles' destruction is his own wife, and indirectly his earlier enemy, Nessus, who misled Deianeira about the 'love potion'. Secondly, Heracles himself does not appear on stage until the very end of the play, so his interactions with his family are for the most part seen through the reactions of his distraught wife. The greatest difference between the two playwrights' stories lies in the attitude of Heracles himself. In Euripides' play the hero is presented as deeply concerned about his family, and inspired by his calamity to reflect on his status and the nature of the universe. In the *Women of Trachis* the hero is far less reflective. From the start of the play we are given an impression of a figure who does not have strong ties to others, leaving his wife and son without information, and then sending Iole on without explanation.[15] (While Megara in Euripides' *Heracles* is similarly unaware of her husband's whereabouts, a reason is soon provided in Heracles' stay in Hades). Fifth-century Athens was a strongly patriarchal society in which women were viewed as inferior to men and had few rights: while there was horror at the prospect of female infidelity, men were relatively free to indulge their sexual passions.[16] The original audience may well have felt that Deianeira over-reacted to her husband's concubine, but the misery of deceit and confusion which opens the play does create a troubled atmosphere. Heracles should perhaps have taken a more active interest in his women in order to maintain a stable household. Furthermore, at the end of the play Heracles' attitude to his family is brusque. His anger at his wife may be understandable, but by ordering his son to marry Iole he is shown as uncaring about his son's feelings. Hyllus protests when he hears his father's command, *Women of Trachis* vv. 1232ff.:

HERACLES: You speak as if you would do none of the things I ask.
HYLLUS: How could anyone when she alone shares
                the blame for my mother's death and your condition?
                How could anyone choose to do that, unless
                avenging fiends had made his mind sick? Better
                for me, too, to die than live with my worst enemy.
HERACLES: I see the man will not give me my due, though I
                am dying. But I tell you, if you disobey
                my commands, the curse of the Gods will be waiting for
                you.[17]

Sophocles' hero in this play is a man with a family, but not really within it. It may be significant that the play opens as his family searches for him, and when he calls for his family at the end of the play they are unable to come. The play is also different from Euripides' *Heracles* in its presentation of the physicality of the hero. As Dunn notes, in the *Women of Trachis* the emphasis is on Heracles' hands, the raw physicality of the man, rather than the bow, which forms such a centrepiece in Euripides' *Heracles*.[18]

Heracles was also a figure in a number of plays known to us today only from fragments and hypotheses, and Huys suggests that in the *Auge* of Euripides Heracles was also shown as a family man.[19] It is possible that *Heracles* was part of a trilogy, which had an earlier episode showing Heracles in Hades, rescuing Theseus and Peirithous. This is the argument suggested by Mette, and persuasively developed by Dobrov.[20]

From the material we have it is difficult to form judgements about the tragic tradition of representing Heracles on stage. Although the character of Heracles does not seem to have been particularly common, the representation of tragic madness was popular, as in Sophocles' *Ajax* and Euripides' *Bacchae*.[21]

Heracles in comedy

The plays which have survived from the fifth century give the casual reader a false picture of the relative importance of comedy and tragedy to their society, and the importance of Heracles as a comic figure. In the words of Galinsky, at the opening of his chapter on Heracles the comic hero: 'The number of serious dramas in which he has a part is a small trickle compared to the torrent of satyr plays, farces and comedies in which Heracles kept entertaining his audiences, and their delight with him does not seem to have known a saturation point.'[22] In the previous chapter we noted the way in which Heracles could be presented as a figure of excess, and there were many possibilities for comedy offered by such a character. Satyr plays seem to have often featured Heracles in major or supporting roles, although, unfortunately, our evidence for these plays is patchy.[23]

Many of the plays presented in the comic competitions ('Old Comedy' in the fifth century) took the form of mythological burlesque where Heracles' many exploits provided obvious plotlines. The only comedies of the fifth century which have survived are those of Aristophanes, and he favoured a particularly literary and political form of comedy, rather than the mythological burlesque. Galinsky provides a complete survey of the evidence which indicates that Heracles was a popular figure in comedy, as, for example, when he is referred to in Aristophanes' *Peace* vv. 741-2.[24] The only really accessible evidence comes from Aristophanes' *Frogs*, the play which stages a literary critique of tragedy as Dionysus descends to Hades to bring back a playwright.[25] In the play we do also see the figure of Heracles, but he is given quite a sophisticated, almost detached role, laughing at the main comic figures of Xanthias and Dionysus. However, Aristophanes' manipulation of the story indicates several of the ways in which we may imagine the figure of Heracles was traditionally deployed. Dionysus and Xanthias decide to dress up like Heracles, and much play is made of physical and visual humour about his strength and appearance.[26] For our purposes in this volume, it is also worth noting that the *Frogs* contains a specific reference to the madness of Heracles, when at vv. 564-8 he is described as waving his sword 'as if mad', and the response is made 'Yes, that sounds like Heracles, all right!'

Two important points can be drawn from this play. Firstly, that Heracles' reputation for madness was a well-established part of his mythology by the end of the fifth century, possibly helped by Euripides' portrayal in *Heracles*. Secondly, that the choice of Heracles as a subject for tragedy was not an obvious one, because he was strongly identified as a comic figure. Tragedy done badly easily slides over into comedy, so an approach to this figure would not have been undertaken lightly by any tragedian.

Euripides and Heracles

Although Euripides' plays did not often win the competitions, his plays were widely known, copied and thus transmitted.[27] The ambiguous popularity of his plays is often seen as a reflection of his innovative and controversial style of tragedy, a particular approach to myth and the medium of drama which distinguished his work from that of his predecessors. He reduced the role of the chorus and pushed the boundaries of dramatic characterisation, exploring social realities, the nature of story and what we today would term the psychology of his characters. His work was easily identifiable to his contemporaries, both in his handling of subject matter and in the style of presentation, in costume, language and music. Characteristics of his style include an increased interest in domestic situations, an awareness of rationalising approaches to myth and religion, a highly reflexive attitude to literary tradition, and a particular skill in the deployment of emotional and psychological effects, both within the frame of the drama itself and in the interaction between audience and actors. Segal argues that Euripides was particularly self-aware in his use of tragedy to manipulate the emotional responses of the audience to highly charged events.[28] This highly distinctive style was recognised and parodied by the great contemporary comedian and critic Aristophanes in the *Frogs*. The comedy stages a competition between the dead Aeschylus and Euripides to determine who is the better playwright (in the context of Dionysus' attempt to use tragedy to restore Athenian morale). The caricatures of each playwright's style are far from reliable evidence, but they do suggest that the broad outlines of Euripidean style were easily recognised by an audience in the late fifth century. The insults thrown at 'Euripides' by 'Aeschylus' focus on his use of lowly characters, such as women and slaves, a lack of heroic flavour, an interest in new philosophical thinking, and a general disregard for maintenance of traditional values.

The *Heracles* displays many of these features: an interest in domestic issues (the voices of the children, the maternal fears of Megara, the pathetic impotence of the old man Amphitryon); a willingness to reframe existing literary traditions to provide a different emphasis (Heracles' family loyalties, the order of events); a complex perspective on the role of the gods, both presenting them as on-stage characters, then having the central figure question their status and reject their authority.[29] These features of Euripides' style may be seen as natural developments of the genre as it evolved over the generations. The original format of tragedy grew out of choral performances with the actors as secondary elements, and this balance of emphasis was generally reversed as the fifth century progressed. It is also the case that tragedy was a part of Athens, created by the city and responding to its changes. Many of the characteristics of Euripidean tragedy are related to new developments in Athens in the late fifth century, from intellectual debates such as those provoked by the sophists, to the grim practicalities of long-drawn out war with Sparta.[30] The city which produced tragedy in the first half of the century was a community battered but proud after the Persian wars. The citizens displayed rising self-confidence, wealth and optimism as Athens grew into an imperial power. By the time Euripides reached adulthood the situation was more complicated, as Athens' onward march faced more challenges and provoked more questions. The democratic system became far more volatile than it had been in previous generations.[31] It is not surprising that the plays produced in this period should reflect such changes, and present a different set of ideas and images from those which were appropriate some fifty years before. However, the nature of Euripidean drama cannot solely be attributed to historical developments, whether in the community of Athens or in the mechanics of literary evolution. The characterisation of Euripides as the 'bright young thing' is somewhat misleading, for he was a near contemporary of Sophocles and the two men were frequent rivals. Sophocles' plays tend to be seen as more traditional, yet he was a product of the same society and open to similar influences to those which may have inspired Euripides' work.

We should also remember that while in many ways tragedy was a traditionally conservative medium, tailored to a ritual context, there was a strand of innovation running counter to this. Innovation was an important force in moving tragedy on from its choral beginnings, and we can see a number of points where particular innovations failed to flourish, such as the increased characterisation of the chorus in Aeschylus' *The Furies*, or moves to dramatise recent historical events such as

Aeschylus' *Persians* or Phrynichus' disastrous *Capture of Miletus*.[32] The distinguishing feature of Euripides' works was perhaps the extent of his innovation and the motivation behind it. His plays display a sustained intellectual engagement with the idea of tragedy as a malleable form, a literary medium able to draw upon its strengths in tradition and its position in Athens to achieve an alchemy of old into new, improving old stories by putting them into new bottles, and transforming style and content in the process. Euripidean tragedy frequently disorientates the audience while apparently presenting a linear narrative, because it questions the very nature of illusion and reality and challenges the viewer to reflect on the act of viewing.

The term *metatheatre* is often applied to this style of drama, and analysis of metatheatrical aspects of tragedy has been one of the most influential approaches to tragedy in recent decades. Metatheatre is defined by Dobrov as 'that process whereby a representation doubles back on itself, where a narrative or performance recognizes, engages, or exploits its own fictionality'.[33] The audience engages in a process of suspended disbelief when they watch a play, and the playwright usually tries to avoid anything which would break that illusion. Metatheatrical works, however, play with the tension between the two levels of knowledge held by the audience, who at one moment both know that they are watching a play, and yet also accept the reality of the events unfolding before them on stage. The original formulation of metatheatre by Abel was more far-reaching, as it spoke of the way fiction can expose the inherent theatricality of life.[34] Metatheatre encourages the audience to contemplate issues about what is real and what is illusion. Greek tragedy did not have access to advanced visual techniques, but the structures of ancient drama, philosophy and religion indicate that the fifth-century Athenians did indeed think about the nature of reality in sophisticated ways. In *The Republic*, Plato distinguished between different levels of experience, suggesting that we are like people in a cave, who see shadows reflected by a fire, and mistake those shadows for the real world.[35] Euripidean drama can be seen as a response to broad intellectual developments, as a product of its time, as much as a product of one individual's vision. Nevertheless, many of the apparently difficult or unsettling aspects of the plays may be read as deliberate features, as the playwright worked to engage his audience in intellectual debate.

Where then, does this leave the *Heracles*? We have already noted a number of typically Euripidean features, such as interest in women and children. Internal evidence dates the play to between 425 and 416 BCE.[36] The late fifth century was a turbulent time, as Athens waged war on several fronts, resulting in social and political instability. The complexities of the mythological figure of Heracles, combined with a complex literary tradition, offered great opportunities to a playwright interested in challenging his audience. Although the play has had its detractors, the range of debates it has inspired indicates that the fundamental paradox of Heracles' story can fascinate audiences, ancient and modern, regardless of any perceived failures of artistic composition. In the following chapter we will examine the techniques of dramatic structure which Euripides employed, and see how the issues raised in this chapter could be manifested in a staged production.

4

Dramatic Structure and Unity

Summary of the play

DRAMATIS PERSONAE

Amphitryon, mortal father of Heracles. An old man.

Megara, wife of Heracles. Daughter of the murdered king of Thebes.

The three young sons of Heracles and Megara.

Chorus of the old men of Thebes.

Lycus, a new tyrant who has seized power in Thebes, killing Megara's natal family.

Heracles.

Iris, messenger of the gods.

Lyssa, goddess of madness.

Theseus, king of Athens.

The start of the play presents the audience with the first of several striking visual tableaux, with Megara, Amphitryon and the three boys huddled around the altar of Zeus the Saviour. Amphitryon's opening speech gives this scene its wider context, beginning with his words about his own situation, as the man who shared his wife with Zeus.

The old man draws the audience into his story through his peremptory self-identification, implying both pride in his fame, and an uneasy awareness of his ambiguous position. He swiftly moves on to outline the family circumstances, telling of Heracles' absence, and the murder of the ruler of Thebes by Lycus, who now threatens to kill Heracles' children. The reason for this threat, which Lycus will himself admit, is that the new tyrant fears that the children would take revenge on him if they grew to adulthood. The focus is immediately centred on the children, and Megara's first words (60ff.) are also concerned with the children, as she reports how her sons pester her with questions. In this opening scene both Amphitryon and Megara express their feelings of helplessness, with Megara openly pessimistic and Amphitryon still clinging to some idea of hope.

The *parodos*. At this point the Chorus of fifteen old men of Thebes enter the *orchêstra*. Their song restates the information we have just received, the danger posed to the family. Their comments emphasise the family's isolation, as the old men are themselves too weak to help. The passivity of the first scenes is contrasted by the arrival of Lycus at 140, probably accompanied by a number of armed servants. He insults Heracles, pours scorn on his achievements, then confirms Amphitryon's earlier statement that he will kill the children to prevent future revenge, an act he calls 'prudent caution'. Amphitryon makes a spirited reply defending his son's reputation and calling Lycus' threat to the children 'cowardly'.

Lycus' response is to order branches to be brought in order to burn the family where they sit at the altar. This would be an act of outrageous sacrilege, as suppliants at an altar were by custom taken to be under the protection of a god; the horrified reaction of the Chorus indicates the extremity of the situation as they vow to defend the family with what little strength they have. The imminent prospect of being burned alive prompts Megara to think of the family's dignity and she agrees that the family will leave the altar. As death seems inevitable, Amphitryon and Megara ask Lycus for two concessions, that they should not watch the children die before them, and that they might be allowed to dress the children in dignified funeral clothes, 'the one gift they can receive from their father's house'. Lycus agrees, and leaves the stage. The family then leave the stage with Megara's parting comment that they will at least retain their honour. Amphitryon's remark is far more bitter, insulting Zeus as an adulterer who deserts his friends.

The first choral ode is exceptionally long and complex for a Euripidean chorus and carries a great deal of weight at this crucial stage in the plot.[1] No help has appeared for the family, and Lycus' scornful words about Heracles seem to be justified. The choral ode tells Heracles' story in detail, outlining some of the major events of his life. This intervention serves to remind the audience of the great figure in the background of this story and heightens audience anticipation for his return. The Chorus close by calling attention to the return of the family, now dressed in dark clothes and wearing wreaths for their own funeral.

As they prepare to die, Megara speaks of her family connections, grieves for her children and prays to Heracles to return from Hades. Amphitryon cries for help from Zeus and closes in bitter despair that all his life has been for nothing. At this lowest point of misery, Heracles is sighted, and welcomed as 'a saviour as great as Zeus'. Heracles' arrival changes the tone and pace of the drama. The family rush to his side, and in the following scene he is quickly apprised of the situation. His response is rapid and forceful. He tells the children to take off their funeral clothes, and plans to attack Lycus without delay. On Amphitryon's advice he decides to take Lycus by surprise, and all appears to be well. The restoration of the family security is physically manifested on stage by the children, who cling to Heracles, and he welcomes this with the assertion 'All men love their children'.

The next choral ode expresses great joy at Heracles' return together with philosophical reflections on youth, old age and virtue. All appears to be well, and the Chorus' hopes are quickly fulfilled as Lycus comes back on stage intending to kill the family. Amphitryon tricks Lycus into entering the palace and we hear his cries as he is killed by Heracles, cries which are welcomed by the Chorus. This ends the first dramatic movement of the play. It has conformed to the pattern of a suppliant drama, where a threat is posed but a saviour arrives in the nick of time.

The action of the story now changes rapidly, as the Chorus are shaken out of their joyful song by the sudden appearance of Iris and Lyssa. Iris explains that Hera has been waiting to attack Heracles, but was unable to do so while he was still performing the Labours. Now that she is free to act she has sent Lyssa, to drive Heracles mad and cause him to kill his own children. Lyssa protests that Heracles has done nothing to deserve this fate, but reluctantly agrees to do as Hera wishes. This brief exchange between the two deities marks the start of a new dramatic movement, and introduces the play's most disturbing questions: what has Heracles done to deserve this? How can Hera act with such violence? Why does none of the gods intervene? The Chorus have given the audience plenty of material to support a positive view of Heracles' character, and their reaction to the divine announcement is one of horror. They see Heracles' downfall as an injury to all of Greece, and comment on the instability of any man's good fortune. Their commentary on the situation is interrupted by Amphitryon's cries from within the house as Heracles is seized by madness. In the space of twenty lines Hera's attack is over, and the rest of the play consists of attempts to make sense of what has happened, by Amphitryon, Heracles, Theseus and the audience members themselves through the Chorus.

Confirmation of the murders comes swiftly with the arrival on stage of a messenger who provides a detailed account of events off-stage. He explains how Heracles was overcome during a sacrifice and believed he was in the house of his enemy Eurystheus. He then set out to kill the children, believing them to be those of his enemy. Megara was also killed as she tried to protect the children, and Heracles would even have killed his father had not Athena intervened. The messenger speech gives a vivid account of the off-stage violence, and concludes by calling Heracles the most wretched of men.

Faced with this news, the Chorus are bewildered. They cast around for any parallel cases in mythology, but can find none, and can only turn to look at the new tableau of Heracles surrounded by the bodies and his grieving father, a powerful reworking of the family tableau which opened the play. Amphitryon and the Chorus lament for the family, and are helpless to respond, just as the family was initially unable to respond to the threat from Lycus. When Heracles wakes he is initially dazed and unaware of his previous actions. Slowly, in a passage of *stichomythia*, Amphitryon brings his son to understand what has happened. When he realises the full horror of his own actions Heracles resolves on suicide, as he cannot see a way to continue his life.

At this point a new saviour arrives, Theseus, king of Athens, the friend whom Heracles rescued from Hades. While he too is shocked by what he sees, Theseus provides Heracles with the support to go on living. He advises him that mortals must endure whatever the gods inflict, and offers him a home and honour in Athens. Heracles is initially reluctant, and delivers a long embittered accusation against the gods. He questions whether the gods we know can really be gods, and reflects on the disaster which has befallen him. Theseus again offers his friendship, a repayment for the help he earlier received from Heracles, and his support is finally accepted. Heracles leaves the stage leaning on Theseus. He tells Amphitryon to bury the children with their mother, and promises to return when necessary to bury Amphitryon himself. His final words assert the value of friendship, and the Chorus close the play with the comment that they have lost the 'best of friends'.

Making sense of the play

The tendency to schematise may be a fundamental human impulse, but we saw in the discussion of mythology that Heracles as a figure eludes easy categorisation. *Heracles* the play has presented a similar challenge to critics, and there is no scholarly consensus about the structure or meaning of the play. This chapter will tackle one of the central questions which have preoccupied critics of the play: does the play hang together? Does it have unity? The majority of critics in recent years have attempted to find some meaning and structure in the play, and we will begin by looking at the structure of the play taken as a piece for performance. This section will also serve as an introduction to the key moment of the drama, with links to more detailed discussions in the following chapters.

However, even to follow the sequential narrative poses several problems. From the broadest perspective, there are two 'stories' in the play. The first story is a suppliant drama where the family is threatened by Lycus and rescued by Heracles. This sort of plot, a threat to suppliants which is removed by a saviour, forms the centre of several tragedies, including Euripides' *Suppliants*. However, *Heracles* moves on to a second story, the madness of Heracles and its aftermath. Within this double story structure there are other episodes which may be taken as boundaries, or sub-headings, such as the killing of Lycus, the arrival of Iris and Lyssa, or the arrival of Theseus.

Modes of interpretation

One broad strand of recent criticism has focused on tragedy as a theatrical production, a piece for performance. Oliver Taplin was one of the first major proponents of this approach, and the majority of work from the 1980s onwards has been influenced by this emphasis on theatricality.[2] The opposite approach, favoured by Simon Goldhill and others, has paid attention to the text as a more complex, literary work where language is central.[3] In a contemplative article, Taplin has considered the nature of this divided approach: 'I shall ask whether we are stuck on a hermeneutic underground train on the Circle Line between theatricality and textuality'.[4] Most recent criticism rejects an absolute polarity, and owes something to both approaches, while some have developed more complex views of performance and space.[5] This volume will work with a number of interpretative stances, and in this chapter we begin with discussions of a performance-orientated view of structure. We will then look at a number of overarching thematic structures which may give the play an overall coherence. The final section will reframe the discussion, to ask whether the search for dramatic unity is ultimately warranted. We will explore a number of approaches which reverse the trend, and focus on the lack of unity as a positive dramatic virtue. However, we must begin with a structure before we start to dismantle it.

Staging the play

Greek tragedies were normally produced by the playwright, in the role of *didaskalos*. For modern directors, this creates a difficulty, as the texts transmitted contain no stage directions.[6] Working with the basic framework of performance conditions outlined in the previous chapter, we will explore the different 'acts' of the play, with attention to the points at which staging decisions make a significant contribution to the wider meaning of the play. Visual aspects can be imagined, with the aid of vase images which represent Greek dramatic scenes.[7] Aural aspects are more difficult to ascertain, although we can make some judgements about overall issues, such as the tempo and style of music.[8]

The family in danger (1-251)

The play opens with the family of Heracles clustered around the central altar, here named by Amphitryon as the altar of Zeus the Saviour, a monument established by Heracles. Amphitryon's words emphasise the simplicity of the picture. The scene is thus set for a traditional suppliant drama, such as we see at the opening of Euripides' play *Children of Heracles*. In this case, however, the altar has a more complicated role to play. Amphitryon's opening words have indicated the family link to Zeus, and we will see when Heracles arrives that, as Zeus has not proved a saviour, the family greets Heracles, calling him as great as Zeus. The opening tableau, then, shows us a family sheltering around a stone monument in place of Heracles himself.[9] The static situation is emphasised by the contrast with Megara's words (73ff.) about the children's earlier, exuberant behaviour, pestering her with questions and jumping up to look for Heracles. We must imagine this to be a scene from an earlier stage in the story, before the danger became so pressing, for the on-stage presence of the children is one of fearful, silent stillness.

The arrival of the Chorus at 107 provides a further opportunity for Euripides to direct the audience's attention to features of the staging, as the Chorus members emphasise the manner of their walk as old men, highlighting their own helplessness. From the words alone we can understand that they have sticks and are huddling together, mirroring the state of the family. The frailty of the Chorus adds to the vulnerability of the family – although they will all accuse Lycus of cowardice, they lack the necessary physical strength to fight back. The first words of the Chorus in the *parodos* hint at the costuming of the play, commenting on the resemblance between Heracles and the children (131ff.) and the fire in their eyes. While the details of eyes would not be particularly visible in the large outdoor theatre, it may be that the children were masked to resemble Heracles, particularly with a similarity of hair colour. If such masking suggested a contrast between the children and Amphitryon and Megara, then the costuming would highlight the attachment of Heracles to his sons, and suggest that in the end Heracles killed a part of himself.[10] Furthermore, similarity to, or difference from, Amphitryon could indicate other aspects of family connection, although Amphitryon's age would probably have been his defining feature. The actor playing Megara would have been masked conventionally with a white face to indicate her gender.[11]

Playing Lycus

The appearance of Lycus is something of a puzzle, for it is likely that he was Euripides' own invention. Lycus is a far more two-dimensional villain than is customary in Greek tragedy, without the sort of mythological life story which could contextualise his role. The only possible set of mythological associations would come from the other more established mythological figure called Lycus, the supposed father of our character. Lycus the elder seized power in Thebes at an earlier stage of the mythological history, so there is a suitable family history for Euripides' Lycus to inhabit. There does not seem to have been any form of costume shorthand for identifying villains, not least because the characters of tragedy are seldom shown in black-and-white terms as entirely good or bad. There are no figures comparable to the cat-stroking villains in dark glasses which we see in modern cinema.

The reason that speculation about the appearance of Lycus is so important is the observance of the three actor rule in tragedy. In this play, the protagonist must have played the roles of Lycus and Heracles, creating a sharp irony. Heracles rescues his family from Lycus only to then inflict the same destruction himself. We cannot know how far the original audience would have been aware of this issue of double roles, but it seems likely that they would have noticed, not least because the protagonist of each trilogy was competing for prizes. It is tempting to speculate how Euripides would have worked with, or against, that process of identification. The play calls for a conventional iconography of Heracles, with lion skin, club and arrows, as these will be the instruments of murder which he thinks of destroying at the end of the play.[12] We should probably imagine that the actor wore padding and possibly high-soled shoes to indicate his great heroic status. It may be that Lycus was portrayed with the opposite appearance, smaller, simpler, relying on words rather than weapons, as would befit a man who prided himself on political pragmatism and despised Heracles' strength. The opposite appearance of Heracles and Lycus would then lead the audience to contemplate how different figures can reach the same outcome, or whether there are deeper levels of similarity, as Krauss has argued.[13] Heracles expresses incomprehension of Lycus' threat to the children, and yet achieves what Lycus had planned with even greater violence. In this way, details of staging can reinforce ideas expressed verbally in the text of the play.

Abandoning hope (252-513)

When Lycus sends his men off the stage (240ff.), the altar acquires a different symbolic meaning – no longer a place of refuge, it will become a pyre as Lycus threatens to burn the family where they stand. It is not far-fetched, therefore, to suggest that the altar is a physical symbol of what Heracles himself will be to the family – a source first of protection, and then of destruction. The staging of these first scenes represents a further tension in the narrative, between the static and the active: should the family try to wait it out until the final moment, hoping for Heracles' return, or should they give in to the inevitable? Amphitryon's movement in abandoning the altar is thus both a consequence of, and a representation of, his decision to meet his fate. The symbolism of supplication is then perverted as Amphitryon offers his throat to Lycus. The deadlock is broken only by Lycus' decision to agree to Megara's request and allow the family to go indoors to prepare for their death. Although Burnett argued that Megara committed an act of *hybris*, by abandoning faith in the altar, the majority of critics would argue that Megara was acting nobly and pragmatically.[14] The family leave the stage, to prepare for their deaths (347), and their action only moves them closer to destruction.

The mood of apprehension is now suspended as the Chorus sing a catalogue of Heracles' Labours. The choral ode is, however, not detached from the action of the play as the old men are reflecting on the only possible source of rescue.[15] Heracles' powerful actions offer a potential solution to the stalemate which the family faces. Furthermore, the tone of the passage modulates the high tension of the previous scenes by directing the attention of the audience to the wider perspective. This in turn reinforces the shock when the action resumes as the family returns, alive, but dressed for burial, probably in white.[16] A similar scene may have been staged in Euripides' *Melanippe the Wise*, as the hypothesis to that play indicates that Melanippe's children were to be prepared for death.[17] One of the great strengths of this play is the manner in which Euripides manipulates the audience response, and the use of choral passages is a crucial element in the balance between action and reflection. The respite for the audience is, however, very brief, for the focus returns to the immediate drama with the Chorus' words (442-50), noting the change in the family tableau. They are huddled together, and the focus narrows still further as Megara reflects on her earlier hopes for the children. The memory of happier times makes the present situation more pitiable, and once again our attention is drawn to the gap which Heracles has left in his family. At this point (498), Amphitryon steps outside the family and we see him for a brief moment not as 'the father of Heracles', but as an old man, isolated, reflecting on his fate.[18] He raises his hands to the sky, receives no response, and then turns to his friends, the Chorus, physically staging what may be one of the underlying messages of the play – rely on friends rather than divine providence. This point in the play is the first *crisis*, in the Greek sense of the word as 'decision time'. The movements of the family have been increasingly restricted, and the only role left to them appears to be that of sacrificial victims. The situation was dark when the play opened, and the two arrivals, of the Chorus and Lycus, have only emphasised the family's despair. The dramatic tension has reached a highpoint when Heracles arrives to save his family, just in the nick of time. It is important to note this standard dramatic pacing, build up to a crisis followed by a resolution, as it provides a counterpoint to the very different dynamic which Euripides brings into play when Heracles is afflicted by madness and kills the children.

Heracles the saviour and family man (514-635)

At this point in the play (514ff.), we may think of the story moving into Act Two. Heracles' arrival presents the director with a number of decisions. Megara sees Heracles approaching from off stage, and tells the children to run to him.[19] The following lines are delivered by Heracles as he greets his home, notices that something is wrong, and announces his intention to draw closer. Kovacs adds a note to his translation at this point (522): 'The action "freezes" for a few seconds (M.'s order is probably carried out at 530) to allow H. to react separately.'[20] This is a plausible staging device, although generally orders given to children and silent characters in tragedy are carried out immediately.[21] The Theatre of Dionysus gave Euripides a reasonable amount of space to play with. The children could run to Heracles once released by Megara, and thus cause Heracles' cry (525), 'What's the matter? Children I see in front of the house' – this literal translation emphasises the word order in the Greek which foregrounds the word 'children'.

However it is staged, the transfer of the children into Heracles' care is significant for the shift in family control. We may imagine that the earlier family tableau with the family at the altar is now recreated with Heracles as its centrepiece.

Heracles asserts his role as family protector and as the strongest figure in the situation, reversing Lycus' orders as he tells the children to take off their funeral clothes. The family unit is now active rather than passive, and the portrayal of Heracles on stage must be one of strong movement. Euripides uses far more comments on movement in his plays than does Aeschylus or Sophocles, a fact which may indicate how his characters struggle to take control of their actions.[22] It is important to note that the previous static language of the family about sight and appearance is now replaced by language of speed and action. The impulse to immediate revenge is tempered by Amphitryon who may well physically try to restrain Heracles. His good sense prevails, and Heracles' immediate violent impulse is checked. The ability of Amphitryon to control Heracles' passion is a significant feature of this scene which will be echoed when the murders occur, and only a god can stop him. At this point, the action of the drama has provided a positive reversal of the earlier scenes, and Heracles leaves the stage with his family, the children clinging happily to him. This is the last time the audience will see Megara or the children alive.

Joy turned to sorrow – Lycus, Iris and Lyssa (637-909)

The exit of the family brings to a close the suppliant drama, with all that remains as the death of Lycus. Two choral passages frame a brief scene as Amphitryon lures Lycus into the house. Off-stage death cries are a traditional feature of tragedy, and in this case they receive immediate welcome from the Chorus who celebrate the death of the tyrant (760-1): 'The godless man is no more, the house is silent. Let us turn ourselves to dancing.' We should imagine that the music at this point is lively and cheerful, the Chorus members dancing, with perhaps some concessions to their characterisation as old men.[23] This mood of happy celebration appears to provide a conclusion to the action, but the mood quickly changes with the arrival of Iris and Lyssa.[24] From their previous exuberance the Chorus now shrink away in fear as the deities arrive. Their intervention is unexpected and decisive. The text of the play makes it clear that the Chorus can see them, so the audience surely will as well, although Kovacs' translation notes that the scenes can be staged with the deities invisible. The two figures probably do not appear on the stage area itself, but in one of two other areas, the *mêchanê* or the top of the stage buildings. The *mêchanê* as the traditional location of gods in tragedy would emphasise the arrival of divine agents, whereas the use of the rooftop would tie in with the play's attention to the physical house.

Wherever they are placed, the sudden appearance of Iris and Lyssa would indicate their divine status, possibly with the use of traditional attributes which would have identified them in art: Iris with a messenger's staff and wings, or winged boots, and Lyssa in hunter's clothing.[25] They quarrel about the madness in one of the central problem passages – we will return to this issue in Chapter 6. As soon as their brief argument is concluded, Lyssa moves into the house, and the pace of the story speeds up dramatically. The audience's attention is now focused on the impending disaster, and within the space of a few lines Amphitryon's cries from off-stage are heard, echoing the earlier cries of Lycus.[26] It is significant that the audience has not seen Heracles after his killing of Lycus, and so what the audience experiences in a short period of time is two cries from off-stage both caused by Heracles. The action moves swiftly on with the arrival of the Messenger, creating a sense of disorientation for the audience as time is speeded up, emphasising how suddenly the world can change. As Higgins discusses, temporal distortion is a central feature of the play, and Heracles himself is not as grounded as he initially seemed.[27]

The Messenger's account of the Madness (910-1015)

The Messenger's speech now gives us a double narrative of actual events and Heracles' delusional perceptions. This is the part of the play which is most strongly metatheatrical. Particular attention is paid to the physical blocking of the scenes which reverse previous actions and tableaux of the play. The Messenger's first description of Heracles and his family at the altar presents a positive counterpart to the play's first scene as Heracles completes the family circle. However, there is a discordant note as the Messenger describes the children as gathered as a 'chorus' (925). Even though they are situated as a chorus, thus conventionally outside the direct action of tragedy, they will be drawn into the drama of Heracles' madness, breaking generic conventions as stories within stories merge into one. Even the intervention of Athena is presented with a detail which draws attention to the narrative process itself, for the Messenger describes her as an *image*, using the terminology often used for works of art (*eikon*, 1002). Figures in tragedy are occasionally compared to works of art, most notably the Pythia's comparison of the Furies to pictures of harpies in Aeschylus' *The Furies*, but the Messenger's use of the statue/art image for something which he describes in powerful *action* highlights the division between fiction and reality. Heracles is not the only one in this scene who is confused about what he's seeing.

The aftermath (1016-end)

The end of the messenger speech is followed almost immediately by the physical manifestation of the scene he described. As Heracles is bound, with the bodies of his children around him, the most likely staging technique would be the use of the *ekkyklêma* to bring an inside scene outdoors. It is also possible that only Heracles is brought on to the stage, and that the bodies of the families are imagined as part of the off-stage scene, visible to the actors but not the audience. Such a staging of the scene might emphasise the isolation of Heracles, as the last time we saw him on stage he was surrounded by his family. Nevertheless, an on-stage presence of the bodies would give a clear focus for Heracles' own distress and a strong visual counterpart to Theseus' comment that Heracles is in the middle of corpses (1189). Whichever solution was favoured, this scene provides a stark contrast to the earlier family tableaux in the play.

Once Heracles has realised his true situation his response is to turn in on himself. He covers his head and wishes that he could be a rock, recalling the myth of Niobe whose children are

killed before she herself is turned to stone, or the figure of
Achilles in his tent.[28] Heracles' wish for death is symbolised by
his act of hiding from sight, and Theseus is initially unable to
recognise him. His decision to live is marked as he lifts his head.
This scene presents the audience with a complicated set of ideas
about identity, character and circumstance. Heracles has
wished to lose his humanity, and become a rock.[29] He is no
longer the family man he was at the beginning of the play, and
yet Theseus frames the change in opposite terms, telling him
that he is talking like an 'ordinary man', forgetting who he is.
The outward symbols of his previous life, his weapons, remain,
but have now taken on a different meaning as the instruments
of his family's murder. This play, which began with the confusion over Amphitryon's role, concludes with an even greater
chaos of identity. Heracles, who arrived like Zeus the Saviour, is
now in need of purification and support; he claims that Theseus
will be like his son from now on, and yet the image he chooses,
that of the *epholkis*, or 'little boat', puts him in the position of
child to Theseus' father. In the final scene Heracles leaves
Amphitryon, Megara and the children on stage, just as they
were when the play began.

This discussion of the staging of the play has indicated how
the blocking of particular scenes can highlight certain aspects of
the story. In the following chapters we will look at the central
issues in detail, but this chapter's discussion of the play's unity
will conclude with brief comment on some of the other inter-
locking themes which Euripides employs. The idea that the play
was held together by textual and thematic links was argued by
Porter, and has been the basic approach adopted by many
recent critics.[30]

Physical links – architecture and yoking

In the following chapter we will look at the issue of family relationships, but it is worth noting that the idea of the physical
house also plays a significant part in the drama. There is a
strong sense of architecture in this play, from the altar of Zeus
to the pillar where Heracles is tied after his madness. When

Megara dresses the children in funeral clothes, they are both symbolically and literally wearing 'all that the house can give them' (329-31), and Lyssa's final words link the physical and metaphorical when she comments that she will 'enter the house unseen' (873). Rehm notes that when Heracles returns, he highlights the building of the house as home, and that Heracles himself is conceptualised as a building.[31] He comments further on the messenger speech and the perversion of the house as protection, as the children 'run to the symbolic cornerstones of the Greek social life – the family, the home and the gods'.[32] A similar confusion of home/house/safety can be found in Euripides' *Medea* when there is constant anxiety about the safety of the children inside/outside the house.

The house/home dynamic is presented on different levels, with the architecture functioning as a physical and metaphorical focus. The family relationships are also represented in different modes, physically represented on stage, and complemented by verbal references. Worman has explored the patterns of yoking and binding which form part of the imagery and the physical staging of the play.[33] The strongest image comes when the family are prepared to die at Lycus' hands and the Chorus describe the scene as the children cling to Megara and she guides them. Megara herself then calls attention to the sight, as 'a pretty yoke of corpses' (454). Ideas of interdependence and connection are, therefore, shown as literal and symbolic within the play, and ideas of connection are shown to be both a source of support and a burden. As Rehm notes: 'Herakles conjoins heroic, paternal and maternal roles as he walks his family home.'[34]

Imagery

One of the strongest structural features of the play which is apparent to readers as well as viewers of the play is the extent to which systems of imagery are used.[35] The first, and perhaps most noticeable, of these is the system of ornithological imagery. The first image occurs early in the play when Megara compares her protection of the children to that of a mother bird for her young (71-2). This image is often used in tragedy, frequently in contexts such as this one, where the words may be matched by a physical gesture on stage, the adult putting an arm around the child. As well as suggesting an idea of the need for protection, the image has a particularly ominous tone for a Greek audience familiar with the Homeric epics. The word for baby bird, *neossos*, occurs twice in Homer. In both cases, the word is used in the context of danger and suffering which suggests its use in tragedy: *Iliad* 2.311 is the omen at Aulis, when a snake devoured a nest of young birds, and *Iliad* 9.323 has the word in the image of a mother bird going hungry to feed her young.[36] The image in tragedy, therefore, is loaded with fear, as the word appears not to be common outside tragedy, and is likely to be a specialised piece of theatrical vocabulary.

From this ominous beginning, the ornithological imagery continues, providing signposts to the significance being placed on the children through six further examples. Amphitryon says that all Greece should help Heracles' children, again describing them as *neossoi* (222ff.). The children are initially characterised as in need of protection from Lycus, but when Heracles returns he changes the focus of the imagery, telling his family 'I am no winged thing' (628). The pattern, however, reasserts itself. As Heracles rages in his madness one of the children hides under the altar like a bird (974), and Heracles himself uses the word *neossos* to describe the child of Eurystheus whom he imagines himself to be killing (982). In the aftermath, the Chorus tell of Procne's killing of Itys (1021ff.), and her subsequent transformation into the nightingale. In the final ornithological image of the play, Amphitryon is described as crying like a bird over a robbed nest (1039). There is a well-defined structure to the imagery creating a cumulative effect. The bird crying over the nest was an old image, with roots in Homer, but it is finally placed in a strategically important position after six related images, which increases the impact it should have on an audience. The ornithological imagery is, therefore, an important structural element in the play as a whole, indicating the relative vulnerability of the different characters at various points in the action.

4. Dramatic Structure and Unity

At the same time, a system of nautical imagery is employed which suggests other ideas, and provides a different pattern in the narrative. The most striking image is that of the *epholkis*, the little boat. This is the image Heracles himself uses to describe the children when they are clinging to him on stage (631-2). It emphasises the close bond between father and sons, and provides a stronger image of protection for the children than Megara could provide with her mother bird imagery. This first use of the image, then, occurs in the first part of the play, the close of the suppliant drama section. The next nautical image comes in a very different context, indicating how far the situation has changed. When Heracles begins to wake after his madness, the Chorus members cry 'Zeus, why did you lead your child into this sea of trouble?' (1086-7), and in Heracles' own first words (1094ff.) he compares himself to a ship tied up. In terms of the imagery, the big ship has survived, but the smaller ones have perished. Once this situation has been fully acknowledged, the play ends with a return to the earlier image of the *epholkis*, indicating both the parallelism between the two actions of the play and the reversal of fortune. Now it is Heracles who compares himself to the *epholkis*, the small boat in the company of Theseus' large ship, as he now needs the support he had earlier given to his sons. The combination of ornithological and nautical imagery creates a framework of ideas which guides the audience through the confusing, violent narrative of the story.

Vision, knowledge and story

The idea of sight is central to tragedy, the term 'theatre' meaning 'a place for seeing', and it is particularly important in this play. The madness takes the form of optical disorientation, as Heracles imagines himself to be seeing one situation while actually being in another. We noted earlier how the Chorus members comment on the resemblance in the eyes between Heracles and his sons, but the image is more complicated than it seems. The children are described as 'gorgon-eyed' (131), but the same adjective is applied to the snakes which attacked Heracles

as an infant (1266), a further example of the inadequacy of dual-
istic thinking.[37] It is in the eyes that the first signs of Heracles'
madness appear, and the Messenger tells us how the children
gazed at him (930-1). Padilla has discussed the issue of sight,
noting the connections between images of sight and the images
of archery in the play, as both archery and sight involve directing
your attention towards an object.[38] Kosak has argued that
patterns of disease create a thematic structure in the play,
beyond the motif of madness itself,[39] and sight is an important
issue in tragedy and myth, often linked to the motif of corrupted
families. Oedipus blinds himself when he discovers his incest,
and Hecuba takes revenge on Polymestor for the death of her
son by killing Polymestor's children before blinding him.
Devereux has detailed the connections between the eyes and the
genitals in Greek thought, which presents blindness as a symbol
of castration, and Steiner notes that blinding and stoning are
structural equivalents as both dull the senses.[40] Assaël has
argued on structuralist lines that the shape of the play is created
by the interplay of light and dark, which can be staged both
physically and metaphorically with light/dark imagery.[41]

Vision is also linked to the status of the story as fiction, and
the status of story within that fiction. It is a metatheatrical
device – if the characters on stage are deceived by what they see,
how can the audience, or, more precisely, the *spectators* of the
story, trust what they are seeing? The issue of storytelling is in
itself significant. In Chapter 7 we will discuss the importance of
Heracles' final outburst when he doubts the truth of stories
about the gods, and even questions their existence. This is a
baffling, disturbing suggestion for the people in the audience
who have previously seen Iris and Lyssa on stage. There are,
however, other elements in the drama which call the audience's
attention to the process of narration/dramatisation in which
they themselves are involved. When Megara tells how the sons
plague her with questions, Amphitryon advises her to tell them
stories, with the express comment, 'Soothe them with stories,
wretched deceptions' (99-100). The idea that stories might be
useful, even if they are not true, is an interesting point for
tragedy, a genre for which many claims of moral authority and a

didactic purpose have been made in antiquity and in modern scholarship. In this play we see that such strategies are appropriate for children, but the great hero comes to reject such ideas at the end of the play, turning instead for support to the physical presence of his friend rather than trust in the 'wretched tales of poets' (1346). Furthermore, the Chorus are unable to find a mythological parallel to provide any comprehension or consolation for Heracles' loss (1016ff.). This would seem to indicate that sometimes events are so difficult to understand that appeals to the cultural storehouse of mythology are of no use. The manner in which this story is told may paradoxically undermine its own status as a drama with relevance to the concerns of its audience – a strategy which would be highly Euripidean, but also extremely unsettling for an audience.

The issue of storytelling is referred to at crucial points in the drama. We should not assume that such an appreciation of literary irony was beyond some of the original audience, for even the earliest Homeric epics display command of sophisticated literary devices and a deep understanding of the power of story. The potential sophistication of this one element of the *Heracles* indicates the multi-layered approach to the drama which Euripides employed. The range of overlapping thematic elements, such as imagery, staging and significant ideas, provides a framework for interpretation. This allows the audience to understand the action of the play on a surface level, while at the same time posing questions about the very process of coming to terms with ultimate horror.

Heracles can be schematised in many ways, and has a basic structure from the continuity of characters, the role of the Chorus etc. However, is it a satisfying unity? Do the thematic links discussed above provide an adequate structure? Do they really hang together as neatly as some would suggest? Why are we even talking about unity?

The problem of unity

As the play progresses our attention becomes increasingly focused on Heracles himself. This in itself provides one element of coherence in the play as Heracles takes centre stage. The absent, much-missed figure at the start of the play becomes the saviour of the family, as great as Zeus himself, then the focus of Hera's anger and the attack of Iris and Lyssa, then the violent subject of the messenger speech, and finally the introspective, bitter figure on the verge of suicide. The progression of the play may have less to do with the narrative elements (suppliant drama, attack, arrival of friend etc.) and more to do with the transformation of Heracles, from his role in the world at large, through his role in his own family, to his final role as an isolated individual in a hostile universe.

Critics in the late nineteenth and early twentieth centuries did not appreciate the episodic nature of the play. Gilbert Murray, the great champion of English-speaking scholarship on tragedy in the early twentieth century, called it 'broken backed'.[42] The proportions of the play and its sudden changes of pace made it difficult to say conclusively 'this is the heart of the story'. What then is this concept of 'unity'? Aristotle, writing in the fourth century BCE, discussed the ideal tragedy, advancing a number of rules for dramatic success in his work, *The Poetics*. He included the famous idea of 'unity', specifying that there should be unity of the action of the play. We may also read into *The Poetics* the so-called Minor Unity of Time, the principle that events should take place over one day.[43] Aristotle's approach to tragedy is prescriptive, rather than descriptive, setting out how the ideal tragedy (in his view) should be constructed, rather than exploring the different ways in which the various playwrights handled their material. He is happy to pass judgement on the poets when they break 'his' rules. However, *Heracles* does conform to these Aristotelian principles of dramatic unity.[44] The action is focused in one place, and on a short series of actions which occurs during one day. The difficulty arises because this play dramatises what could be seen as two separate stories, the suppliant drama with the threat from Lycus and the subsequent revenge of Heracles, and then the madness of Heracles itself. The dramatic tension of the play ebbs and flows, with sudden changes of pace and focus. We see this most clearly in the role of the Chorus – at several points in the play the main subject of their song is overtaken by events on stage, forcing them to react to a new situation.

Should we then take this play to be a two-for-one story? In many ways, Euripides works hard to keep the audience with him, carefully modulating the dramatic tension. As we discussed in the previous chapter, Euripides was famous for producing a style of drama which pushed the boundaries of the genre and frequently disturbed his audience. His style of drama is highly self-reflexive, inviting the audience to reflect on their own experience in the theatre and the wider issues of illusion and reality. *Heracles* is a play with a well-developed system of visual and verbal links to establish dramatic coherence, and yet it also contains jarring moments where the plot line changes direction and the Chorus, characters and audience are wrong-footed. It may be that the play's awkward structure is a deliberate ploy which ties in with wider themes of reality, story and truth, and that Euripides was deliberately leaving raw edges to the story to unsettle the audience, a mark of his literary skill rather than of dramatic incompetence. This has been the sort of approach adopted by many recent critics. Dunn has argued that the multiple endings of the play are a deliberate dramatic device, and talks of the importance of frustrating the audience's desire for structure and an ending:

> … the plot of *Heracles* negotiates a series of ending: the spectator is implicated in a play with expectations of closure, time after time reaching an apparent end, only to find it is part of a larger, unfriendly story.
>
> Dunn, 'Ends and Means', p. 84

This reading is rejected by Papadopoulou, who argues that there is a real sense of closure at the end of the play.[45] Krauss has suggested that the dramatic logic is one of supplementation or multiplication of motifs, as with the similarities between Heracles and Lycus, or the linguistic play with the alliteration of *tekna kteinein*, to 'kill children'.[46] Rehm has argued that the play asserts the impossibility of creating meaning through the structure of the choral songs. The Chorus begin by dancing, but

63

their dance is replaced by the maddened dance imposed on Heracles by Hera. Finally, the Chorus are absent, indicating human inability to comprehend the actions portrayed: 'Their symbolic absence in the closing scenes of the drama suggests that the lyric adequate to the experience of Heracles has yet to be written.'[47]

Chapters 5 to 8 will each focus on key problems within the play, looking at different frames. We begin with the family relationships, with particular attention to the initial suppliant drama. The following section explores the scenes from the arrival of Iris and Lyssa to the messenger speech telling of the madness itself. In this section we will explore the central problem of the reason for Heracles' suffering. The next chapter will look at the aftermath, with particular attention to Heracles' contemplation of suicide and his rejection of conventional theological thinking. In Chapter 8 we return to issues of unity and closure, by exploring the final part of the play, and the role of Theseus and the relationship of Athens to the story of Heracles.

5

Family Values

All mankind loves children (636)

One of the most notable features of the play is the depth and complexity of the family relationships. In Sophocles' *Women of Trachis* individual family members appear to have only superficial contact with each other.[1] Euripides, however, delineates strong bonds between Heracles, his father, wife and children, and the concept of *philia* (love or affection) is central to the play's dynamics.[2] This chapter will consider three interrelated topics, beginning with a brief analysis of Greek ideas about family and genealogy. The central section explores the family dynamics through the individual relationships. Finally, we will look at the issue of family, the community, and warfare as expressed in the debate on the bow.

Greek ideas of 'family'

There is no single Greek word which corresponds exactly to the English 'family'. The closest word is *oikos*, usually translated as 'household/family'.[3] For fifth-century Athenians, the word implied a unit comprising individuals linked by blood or marriage, but also referred to a network of financial associations which ensured the transmission of property down the generations. The adult male formed the head of the *oikos* in the role of *kurios*, or 'governor'. This term indicated legal control over boys until they reached the age of maturity, and over all women in the family, including those brought into the *oikos* by marriage. The *oikos* was also the focus for the obligation of *tropheia*, 'nurture': as parents cared for their children, so the children in turn had an obligation to care for their elderly parents. This responsibility was seen as a religious ritual as well as a moral obligation, and due to its value to society the institution of *tropheia* was protected by a number of laws.[4] As Barone has demonstrated, childlessness was both a biological and a social problem.[5]

In Athens the *polis* actively supported the institutions of the *oikos* and assumed its functions when no suitable male relative was available after a death – the city appointed legal guardians for heiresses and fatherless children. The city also provided for children whose fathers were killed in war, as a demonstration of the relationship between individual and state.[6] The literature of the fifth century appears to indicate that there was growing debate over the relative responsibility of an individual towards his family and towards his city-state. There existed an ideal relationship between the two, where the demands of each structure coincided. Conflicts arose, however, particularly in times of war. Consider two examples of this from the fifth century, one from drama, and one from a historical account. Sophocles' play *Antigone* dramatises the continuation of the myth after the sons of Oedipus have killed each other. Their uncle, Creon, has become king and decreed that the one brother, Polyneices, should not receive burial. His decree is defied by Antigone, who believes that it is right to honour both of her brothers with burial. Antigone claims the primacy of loyalty to family over loyalty to state, whereas Creon puts the state first. In the play it is Creon who is ultimately proved to be in the wrong, and who is condemned by the gods, but we can see a similar rhetoric of loyalty to the state in Thucydides' account of a speech given by the statesman Pericles in 430 BCE:

> My own opinion is that when the whole state is on the right course it is a better thing for each separate individual than when private interests are satisfied but the state as a whole is going downhill. However well off a man may be in his private life, he will still be involved in the general ruin if his country is destroyed: whereas, so long as the state itself is secure, individuals have a much greater chance of recovering from their private misfortunes.[7]

Despite these issues, the *polis* and *oikos* had a symbiotic relationship, and the debate is more complex than at first appears. For the purposes of this present discussion, it is enough to note that the *oikos* structure headed by the adult male was still for most practical purposes the model for the fifth-century Athenian family. The structure may, however, have been problematised by particular historical developments. While the *oikos* formed the family unit most familiar to the original audience of the play, the families of mythology did not always display such a precise formal structure. The divergence between social reality and mythical society can be seen in tragedy from a number of angles. The main characters are often of the mythological royal families, where different preoccupations about family power and the relationship to wider society are seen to operate. Mythological stories often involve women wielding considerably greater power than a fifth-century Athenian household would find acceptable – this too may reflect the royal status of the characters, or it may reflect the portrayal of exceptional women in negative contexts, which may reinforce the societal norms of the audience.[8] A final point is that mythological stories do not often involve rituals of society, such as initiation rights, but may rather provide explanations, *aetia*, for them or express underlying anxieties.[9] This is particularly true of tragedy's handling of myth. The original audience of *Heracles* had two sets of family patterns to draw upon, one from their own daily lives and one from the inherited body of myths which belonged to the wider culture.

Such a dual perspective is also needed when considering the issue of genealogy. Ideas of generational continuity were prominent in Greek mythology, and in the family practices of Athens. Children were seen as links to ensure the survival of the family, for care of the elderly, control of finances, and the upkeep of family tombs, cults and reputations. Family history linked up to mythology if the line could be traced back far enough. Links to famous ancestors had considerable political currency in the fifth century, in terms of forging alliances and determining political standpoints. It is, therefore, understandable that there was great interest in mythological genealogies, and one of the earliest surviving works of literature, Hesiod's *Theogony*, forms a genealogical baseline for Greek society starting from the stories of the gods.[10] The importance of genealogy for fifth-century audiences provides a context for Amphitryon's opening words in the *Heracles*, so we will begin the analysis of family relationships in the play with that between Heracles and his father.

Heracles and Amphitryon

Amphitryon's opening prologue both emphasises the continuity of his family line and obliquely indicates the threat of destabilisation. The genealogy which Amphitryon provides shows his pride in his heritage, and his concern to establish his identity through his lineage and to continue the family line through Heracles and his sons. Within Amphitryon's story, however, we see two problems facing the family structure, a temporary instability and a fundamental crisis over Heracles' parentage.

The opening account of the family tree situates Heracles as the son of Amphitryon and Alcmene, but at the same time indicates the other version in which Heracles is the son of Zeus. This apparent contradiction is present throughout the play, culminating in Heracles' final rejection of Zeus as his father on the grounds that true parents do not neglect their children (1264-5). The narrative of the play does not assert any consistent view that Heracles is the son of one or the other. Rather, the idea is posed that Heracles has two fathers. This is not the same issue as raised in modern debates about the roles of biological or adoptive parents, although adoption was possible in Athens.[11] It is instead a feature of Greek mythological thinking which could allow apparently contradictory material to co-exist. As Ebbott has shown, Helen suffers similar problems about ambiguous/dual parentage, as daughter of Zeus or Tyndareus.[12]

This, then, shows us one possible fracture line in the family structure. If Zeus is Heracles' father, then Amphitryon has no link to the next generation of 'his' family, and the long line of ancestors which he traces will end with him. The confusion of

5. Family Values

Amphitryon's role is one of the most interesting features of this play with regard to Heracles' identity as a mortal.[13] In classical Greek societies, a son's identity was formed through his father's identity, from the acceptance of the infant into the family shortly after birth, through the use of family names, and the assumption of adult status through admission to the father's community and the identification of a man as 'X son of Y'. However much Heracles is the exemplar of physical virtues, his social identity rests on an unsure foundation, which in turn raises questions about his own family links with his children. On a psychological reading, Griffith has suggested that Heracles kills his children because of transferred violent urges towards his father.[14]

The second threat which Amphitryon contemplates in the prologue is related to his ambiguous role in the family, but only as a temporary problem. He tells us that when Heracles left he asked him to take care of Megara and the children. This situation would be rather unusual by Athenian standards, but not necessarily remarkable in mythological terms. Heracles did not know of the threat to come from Lycus, and Thebes was Megara's family home, where she could expect the protection of male relatives from her natal family. We may imagine that Heracles assigned his family to Amphitryon's care as a symbolic act of respect, rather than with any expectation that he would need to assume an active responsibility for them. Nevertheless, in light of Lycus' actions, Amphitryon's words imply that Heracles' action in placing him in charge of the family was inappropriate and poses a threat to the very existence of the family. To describe the role which has been forced upon him he uses two startling terms, *trophos* and *oikouros*, 'nursemaid' and 'housekeeper' (45). Both of these terms were conventionally applied to women, and indicated that such roles were not suitable activities for a man.[15] Amphitryon's own estimation of his role is highly negative. At first glance the words seem to imply that Amphitryon is both denigrating his own role and accusing Heracles of having deserted him. It soon becomes clear, however, that his dismay comes from the wider situation, and his frustration at his own powerlessness. Unable to prevent

Lycus from seizing power, Amphitryon is now as much a help-less victim as are his charges, Megara and the children. In tragedy the old are often compared to children, with particular reference to their lack of physical strength.[16] Here Amphitryon points up the irony of the situation, noting that the children are too young to help and that he could have helped them if he were younger (230-5).

Although Amphitryon is Heracles' strongest supporter throughout the play, the way in which Euripides has structured the opening prologue does seem to indicate a possible criticism of Heracles for having left his family without a proper adult male figure, as the previous protection of Megara's other relatives is not mentioned. Nevertheless, Amphitryon does not criticise his son, and we see in the opening scenes that there is a strong bond between the two men, despite the issue of parentage. Heracles' absence is attributed to filial duty, the attempt to reclaim a family home in Argos/Tiryns. Amphitryon strongly defends his son against Lycus' accusations of cowardice (170ff.), and makes a spirited attempt to stand up to the tyrant and argue his case. Even when it appears that the end is at hand, Amphitryon expresses his faith in his son. When Heracles does arrive, he reciprocates that trust by taking Amphitryon's advice to kill Lycus by stealth. Thus the opening sections of the play develop a strong relationship between father and son, while still hinting at problems on a structural level. Griffith notes that although this father–son relationship is one of the few positive relation-ships shown in tragedy, there are dark undercurrents.[17]

The father–son dynamic is developed further in the later stages of the play, when the murder of the children is narrated by a messenger, a device common in tragedy to report off-stage deaths. It is, however, through the reactions of Amphitryon that the audience most vividly experience the murder. The old man suffers the violence at first hand, and is only himself saved by the intervention of Athena, a strong comment on the impor-tance of the father–son relationship. In the aftermath, Amphitryon is the one who confronts his son with his actions, much as Cadmus deals with Agave in Euripides' *Bacchae* when she has killed her son Pentheus while possessed by a Dionysiac form of madness. At Heracles' hands, the old man here suffers the fate he had earlier feared from Lycus, watching his grandsons die in front of him, a sight he had described as *anosios* (323), unholy, impious. Amphitryon's reaction to Heracles as he wakes, a mixture of horror and compassion, provides a subtle snapshot of the parent–child relationship. Despite the superhuman violence which Heracles has displayed, his father still responds to him in a human manner. The portrayal of this father's emotions has far greater depth than that of the relationship between Heracles and his own children.

The final scenes of the play push Amphitryon to one side, while simultaneously strengthening his position as Heracles' father. Once he has learned the truth of his actions, Heracles turns in on himself and cuts himself off from Amphitryon. While he rejects the paternity of Zeus, he also fails to respond to his mortal father. What rescues Heracles is not his family structure, but his friendship with Theseus. Just as he had opened the play by noting his own anomalous position, so Amphitryon closes it with a final illustration of the family paradox. Even though it is Heracles who has lost his children, it is Amphitryon who asks 'Who will bury me?'. One of the most important obligations of *tropheia* was for a child to provide burial for his parents, and here we see the motif twice inverted.[18] Firstly, Heracles gives orders for the burial of his own children, and then Amphitryon, who still has a living son, questions whether he will receive that service. This brief cry, and Heracles' reply that he will return to bury him, indicates that Heracles has all but lost his family structure. Amphitryon, who opened the play by situating himself in a proud genealogy, closes the play having lost the hope of descendants, and struggles to achieve the most basic of social obligations. Heracles will not remain to provide support for his father's old age, but will return to bury his body. While Heracles leaves with the friendship of Theseus and the promise of a place in Athens, Amphitryon is left completely isolated with only the thought of a decent burial to console him. Thus, although Athena prevented Amphitryon's death, he has been left an existence which is empty. Heracles' failure to provide adequate *tropheia* for his own father may be related to the fact that he himself as a child was capable of protecting himself from the snakes which Hera sent to kill him (1265ff.). As obligations of *tropheia* were based on a reciprocal arrangement, Heracles, who has never required support, is unable to give it.[19] Father–son relationships have been seen by many critics as central to the play, with the interaction between Heracles and Amphitryon, Heracles and Zeus, and Heracles and the children providing a multi-layered, intergenerational locus for the negotiation of issues of identity.[20]

Heracles and the children

Compared to the glaring difficulties of Heracles' relationship with his father(s), the relationship with his own children at first sight seems unproblematic. Euripides creates a remarkable portrait of an affectionate father and his loving sons which is unparalleled in Greek tragedy. We hear that the children are eager for their father's return and question their mother repeatedly about his absence (73-6).[21] Megara describes how Heracles used to play with the children in happier times, letting them handle his weapons and speculating on their future lives (460ff.) When Heracles finally arrives, this close relationship is presented physically on stage, as the children cling to their father, and he explicitly comments on their actions, comparing the children to the small boats which belonged to a ship's company as supply vessels or lifeboats.[22] The whole passage contains a degree of open affection for children which is not found elsewhere in extant tragedy.[23] This *philoteknia*, love of children, is not an obvious characteristic of the mythological figure of Heracles, as we discussed in Chapter 2. Euripides goes to great lengths to build up his picture of Heracles the family man, showing us not only the father's attitude towards his sons, but also their responses to him, which we should assume to be free of any pretence. The attachment of the children continues right up to the moment when he kills them. The Messenger describes how, when the madness first struck, the children gazed at their father, and one of the sons attempted to reason with Heracles (986ff.) This scene is one further element in the complex portrayal of family relationship in this play. The value which Heracles places on his children is a crucial point in Euripides' version of the story, for it explains the reason for Hera's methods, to strike Heracles where it most hurt, and it adds credibility to the closing portrait of Heracles as a broken man on the verge of suicide. The affection which he feels for his children is a central feature of 'Heracles the mortal', summed up in Heracles' famous assertion of his place in mankind, 'All mankind is child-loving' (636).

However, there are indications in the play that Heracles' relationship with his children is not all that it appears to be. The play contains a number of unsettling thematic parallels: the ways in which Heracles kills the children with the same weapons he had earlier allowed them to play with; the fact that the killing of the children specifically reverses Heracles' earlier action in bringing up Cerberus from Hades – now he will send his children down, in Iris' words (833ff.). The major difficulty, however, stems from the apparent simplicity of his direct assertion (636), 'All mankind is child-loving'. In the Greek there is an ambiguity in the phrase. It could mean 'Everyone loves children', in a universal sense of the place of children in society, or it could mean 'Everyone loves *their own* children', confining the goodwill to their own offspring with no necessary extension of goodwill to anyone else's children. This ambiguity is important in the play because of the nature of the delusion which Hera imposes on Heracles. On one reading of the play, as we will see in Chapter 6, it is basically an optical illusion which changes the nature of the individuals and surrounding which he 'sees'. He believes that he is in the house of his enemy Eurystheus, and so sets about killing what he believes to be Eurystheus' family: there is no suggestion that the violence is un-Heracles-like, except in its mistaken target. Indeed, the violence which is used against Lycus foreshadows these murders. We are, therefore, alerted to the possibility that Heracles does not 'love children' in a general sense, since he is happy to kill someone else's. The language which he uses makes it clear that he 'sees' his victims still as helpless little children, for he describes them as *neossoi*, baby birds (982), the image previously used by Megara to describe her own children (72). This feature of the murders does not suggest that Heracles did not have genuine affection for his *own* children, but it does perhaps suggest that his basic line of work sits uneasily with a family role. There are several examples in Greek literature which recognise that a man might need to adopt different roles which might appear contradictory, as when the warrior Hector returns to greet his infant son in the *Iliad* Book 6; the father must fight to protect his family, but in doing so must leave them. In *Heracles*, however, the direct expression 'Mankind is child-loving' is particularly striking, and resonates through the murder scene. The imagery of the play also highlights this feature, particularly in the use of nautical imagery, which we noted in the previous chapter. The scene of Heracles with his sons attached like little boats is reversed at the end of the play when Heracles sees himself as a little boat, but also when Amphitryon describes Heracles as 'tied up like a shipwreck' as he sleeps after the madness. The big ship had destroyed itself and its company.

Thus, it is through his relationship with his sons that we see Heracles the mortal with human affections who is devastated by the loss he suffers, but we also see him as a man who is willing to use violence against children. This brings him into the company of other figures in tragedy who are violent towards children and who are cast in a negative light because of it, such as Medea in Euripides' *Medea*, Menelaus, the Spartan villain of Euripides' *Andromache*, or Lycus himself in this play who calls his threat to the children 'pragmatic'. In this play, Rivier notes that Heracles' sense of dishonour at the end of the play is greater than his paternal grief.[24] The situation is far from straightforward, and the Chorus of *Heracles* cannot find a suitable parallel for Heracles' tragedy (1014ff.). The choral intervention serves to highlight Heracles' distance from mortal society, and indicates the failure of myth to answer its own questions.

Heracles and Megara

Throughout the play Megara is very much an adjunct to the children, who form the major focus of attention. At the start,

Lycus wished to kill the boys, to prevent them from taking revenge when they grew up. Megara was simply an inconvenience. When Heracles returns he focuses on the children, and in his madness Megara is only killed by accident as she tries to protect one of her sons (998-1000). In Heracles' final remarks Megara is described almost as a funeral casket for her sons, as the burial is described (1361-2), 'Lay the children on their mother's breast, wrap her arms around them.' Nevertheless, Megara's role does provide some crucial links within the story, and indicates more of the fracture lines within the family unit. It is also worth noting that Megara is an unusual female character in tragedy. The roles of women have been often debated by scholars, questioning why tragedy shows so many powerful women on stage, while in fifth-century society they were expected to take a passive, secondary role. A frequent answer has been that the stories of tragedy dealt with male anxieties about female power, and explored what could go wrong when women were not adequately controlled. Hall has formulated the issue as follows:

> ... there is undeniably a tendency towards plots with disruptive women: one generic pattern relating to male–female relations does draw together a large number of the plays and can be taken as an aesthetic expression of a defining feature of the Athenian male's world view. This plot pattern can be formulated as follows: women in tragedy only become disruptive (that is, break one of the 'unwritten laws', act on an inappropriate erotic urge, or flout male authority) in the physical absence of a legitimate husband or *kurios*.
>
> Hall, 'The Sociology of Athenian Tragedy', pp. 106-7

However, as Hall notes, Megara is one of the exceptions to the pattern, in that she continues to behave well even in the absence of her *kurios*, Heracles. She is, therefore, an interesting example of how women can be shown to react independently, without being portrayed in an entirely negative light. Questions have been raised about the way Megara accepts defeat and agrees to Lycus' demands, but her behaviour is invariably rational and honourable. She is strongly focused on the position of the children and her role as mother. While she expresses her fear and grief about the situation, as does Amphitryon, when all appears lost she thinks primarily of the family honour, and resolves that the children should at least have a worthy funeral. It is certainly true that such a focus on honour is a traditionally male characteristic, and that women in tragedy can be condemned for excessively male attention to their own status, the prime example being Medea who expresses the explicitly male desire to be one who 'can harm enemies and do good to friends'. However, Megara is not thinking of her own honour in this situation but that of her family, and in the eyes of the fifth-century audience that can only have been a positive feature. The fact that she is eclipsed as a focus of attention by her children would also mark her as a good woman in the terms of Pericles' Funeral Speech, a woman who is least talked about for praise or blame (Thucydides, *History of the Peloponnesian War* 2.46). The contribution of Megara as the good wife and mother is important for our appreciation of Heracles' own role. Not only did he have a family, he had a good family structure. His wife was honourable, was concerned for the children, and fostered a strong relationship between him and his children.

How then should we interpret Heracles' attitude towards his wife? This is difficult to judge, which is not entirely surprising. Greek ideas of marriage did not involve any necessary meeting of minds, and husband and wife had different spheres of activity in the household.[25] When the wife was fulfilling her role well, as Megara does, there was little need for comment. Heracles does, however, engage in conversation with his wife on his return, acknowledging her position in the family. This is unlike the return of Agamemnon in Aeschylus' *Agamemnon*, where the hero addresses his opening remarks to the country and chorus, and is dismissive of his wife, Clytemnestra, with ultimately disastrous consequences. Furthermore, Megara has a place at the family ceremony which precedes the madness. She is still presented as linked to the children, but is not isolated. While the central structure of the play focuses on the male relationships in the family, Megara maintains a presence as a respected woman, which provides a strong contrast with the divine femininity of Hera. Megara is a positive figure of motherhood, while Hera acts as the hostile stepmother, a motif which is common in Greek mythology though less so in tragedy.[26] Although the story centres on ideas of paternity, the idea of motherhood also has a part to play.

Amphitryon, Megara and the children

The initial family group in the play consists of Amphitryon, Megara and the children, facing a common threat in the absence of Heracles, their *kurios*, and then reacting with shared joy when he returns. This shared status as victim is then repeated when Heracles attacks the family. In the first situation Heracles' absence leaves a gap in the family, and in the second he appears as an intruder into his own family.

The children have a strong identity as a group of three at the start of the play, reinforced by Megara's description of their earlier games with Heracles. This group identity would have been visually powerful on stage, both in the static tableau as the play opens and when the children cling to their father on his return. The children may also have been masked to resemble Heracles, and the Chorus comment on the family resemblance, noting how the children have Heracles' eyes (131ff.). It is significant that the group of three is split only by Heracles himself, and that each child's death is described in a particular vignette by the Messenger. The children are closely linked to Megara, with the image of baby birds under her wing, and she dies while trying to protect them. In another of the play's reversals, Megara initially hands the children over to Heracles' care, urging them to 'run to your father', but her final act is to try to take her son away from Heracles and assume the protective role herself. The relationship between the children and Amphitryon is mediated through his relationships with Heracles and Megara. He advises Megara on the best course of action, but ultimately is in the same situation as she is. He takes on the protective role, however weakly, in response to his son's request. At the start of the play the relationship between Amphitryon and Megara highlights the power vacuum left by

Heracles as they each struggle with their weak positions –
Amphitryon is weak because of age, and Megara because she is
a woman (an obvious fact for a Greek audience!). Neither one is
stronger than the other, and as the action progresses we witness
a change in the relationship. At first it is Megara who is at a
loss, and Amphitryon advises calm and hope, telling her to focus
on distracting the children. After Lycus' threat, however, it is
Megara who takes the initiative, resolving to salvage what
dignity she can from the situation and negotiating directly with
Lycus. Despite their best efforts the family cannot survive
without Heracles, which indicates the irony as he becomes the
source of the family's destruction.

The death of children

The vulnerability of children is socially encoded in various ways
in Greek society. They are often linked to women, as forming
'the other' of the ideal Greek adult male, and there is little
evidence of a sentimental view of childish behaviour. Rather,
childhood is often viewed as an awkward stage which must be
passed through, and the ignorance and weakness of children are
qualities to be avoided. However, children are very important to
individuals and to societies, and are therefore a focus of great
attention and concern. The murder of children in modern societies is often treated as the greatest type of atrocity, and there
is some evidence for this attitude in the ancient world. The
Thracian murder of school children is related with horror by
Thucydides, *History of the Peloponnesian War* 7.29, as being the
greatest atrocity of the war.[27] However, in mythology the killing
of children is more ambiguous. It can be the act of a villain,
acting with pragmatism, as Lycus in this play, or Menelaus in
Euripides' *Andromache*, but it can also be a sensible move. The
death of Astyanax after the fall of Troy can be presented as a
sudden, brutal act, but also as a deliberate, strategic decision.[28]
The failure to kill the baby Paris (Alexandros) leads to the fall
of Troy, and the failure to kill the baby Oedipus leads to the
widespread destruction of his family.[29] Although Lycus is
presented as a villain in this play, the actions which Heracles

thinks he is performing when mad, the killing of Eurystheus' children, could be framed as the pragmatic acts of self-preservation. We will return to this question in the next chapter.

Lycus and the debate on the bow

Lycus presents the first immediate threat to the family, in his desire to crush any future retribution when the sons of Heracles reach adulthood (the dynamic most famously seen in the return of Orestes to avenge Agamemnon). However, he threatens more than their physical safety, questioning their identity and status, when he calls into doubt Heracles' reputation (*doxa*, 157). His assertion that Heracles' achievements are not all they are cracked up to be downplays the significance of all the Labours and casts Heracles as a coward. The centrepiece of his argument is that Heracles has not engaged directly, but hidden behind his bow, which has allowed him to keep a safe distance from danger. The reply from Amphitryon rejects this argument, and the Chorus' glorification of Heracles' Labours supports the more positive view. However, we should not dismiss Lycus' comments as empty words, and considerable attention has been paid by critics to the debate on the bow. The weapon itself comes into play when Heracles kills his children, and is a physical focus on stage when Heracles contemplates rejecting his weapons at the end of the play.

The bow in this story has been seen as representative of the place of the individual in warfare, and has provoked conflicting interpretations. Foley argues that it symbolises a traditional, individual style of heroism, with Heracles as an old-style hero.[30] By contrast, Michelini suggests that the bow indicates a newer, sophisticated heroism.[31] Dunn rejects both views, arguing that the symbolism of the bow is problematic, and has been emptied of meaning.[32] He quotes the comparable passages from the *Iliad* where archery is criticised: Aeneas taunts Pandarus, *Iliad* 5.171-8, 204-16, and even the gods are involved when Hera taunts Artemis, *Iliad* 21.483, 91. The debate is summarised by George who argues that the symbolism of the bow is part of a more intricate set of associations within the play. The bow is 'a visual manifestation of many of the play's issues ... especially independence, dependence and friendship'.[33] The archer/hoplite debate can be framed as a conflict between individual and community, and George notes the irony that Amphitryon rejects community (by valuing the bow), while Lycus champions it.

A further note is introduced by Ebbott, who argues that the archery debate implies the illegitimate status of Heracles.[34] The role of the *nothos* (bastard) may be seen in the context of other mythological illegitimate children, such as Hippolytus, who have similarly complicated family dynamics. The idea of the bow can be seen as linked to ideas of family and community on many levels in this play, and Lycus' verbal attack on the bow complements his physical attack on the family at the altar.

6

Violence and Madness

The death of Lycus and the role of song

As the suppliant plot is concluded and the family goes into the house, the Chorus sing in praise of Youth. The short section of the play between verses 637 and 814 acts as a transition between the two 'stories' in the play, but is far more than a simple plot device, containing ironic juxtapositions. The Chorus' praise of Youth, with the suggestion that the gods should reward the virtuous by giving them a second youth, is appropriate to the myth of Heracles. His return from Hades is a comparable renewal of life, and after his death Heracles will be credited with the power to rejuvenate the old (as happens in Euripides' *Children of Heracles*). However, this sort of wish, an *adynaton* (impossibility), is often seen in tragedy in ominous circumstances: for example, the wish that children could be produced without the need for women is expressed by other Euripidean characters, notably Jason (in *Medea*), and Hippolytus (in *Hippolytus*). Both characters eventually suffer horribly at the hands of the women in their lives (Medea and Phaedra). The idea that the natural order could be reversed to reward virtue provides an ironic counterpoint to the events which so quickly follow in *Heracles*.

The off-stage death of Lycus is presented in the tradition of the death of Agamemnon in Aeschylus' *Agamemnon*, a cry from off-stage which provokes comment, but no intervention, from the Chorus on stage.[1] After his opening cry, Lycus dies with only one line, the ironic 'O land of Cadmus, I am destroyed by deceit' (754). The obvious response made by the Chorus is that he is 'hoist with his own petard'. We could also compare the motif of

81

deceit versus physical force often seen in Greek thought, as, for example, when Odysseus advises Neoptolemus to achieve his aim with deceit rather than force.[2] Heracles' behaviour in myth is often characterised by violence, but he is here following Amphitryon's advice. We recall that, in this version of the myth, Heracles is serving Eurystheus out of filial piety, but that Amphitryon's exile is due to his own act of violence.

The Chorus members are delighted by Lycus' death, and their response is highly self-reflexive, commenting on their role. After their previous remarks about their determination to sing despite their age, they now place Lycus in a context of song. Firstly, there is the idea that the cries they can hear from the palace are the 'songs they love to hear' (751-2), and then the idea that Lycus spread a story, *logos*, that the gods were weak' (757-9). The story turns in on itself, as the fictional characters of the drama are aware of their own position as singers.

Their song glories in Heracles' achievements, and marks him as a man favoured by the gods. Their final comment, that the gods take pleasure in just conduct (811-14), is noted by Bond as a well-crafted phrase:

> ... men raise tentatively the question 'whether the gods still favour a just cause'. There is also a certain ironical litotes in the enunciation, for the gods' action to help the just has been crushing. 'That will show men whether the gods approve of justice', says the intellectual theist with mild nonchalance on hearing that his unjust enemy has been annihilated.[3]

The defeat of Lycus has been presented as an unequivocal success, and a clear demonstration of principles of divine justice. However, the apparent clarity of the situation (emphasised by the vocabulary of vision/showing/appearing, *phainei* 811) is immediately shown to be false, as it is not an abstract principle which appears, but the figures of Iris and Lyssa. From being the ones to respond to Lycus' cries, the Chorus members themselves are the ones to exclaim in terror (*ea ea* 815), when they see the gods appear. Although they refer to the sight as an apparition (*phasma* 817), the gods will wreak havoc just as decisively as Heracles punished Lycus. The sudden reversal of fortune comes just over half way through the play and jars the audience. The movement of the story has taken them from fear for the family, to relief at the return of Heracles, and to triumph at the defeat of Lycus. Now, the story returns to a climate of fear, and this time the impact on the audience will be more direct. Instead of fear/sympathy for the family, the audience experiences something of the sense of disorientation which the characters feel, as they face this unexpected development. This twist in the story is very cleverly designed, and the constant references to sight draw in the audience as spectators, inviting them to reflect on their own role in the situation. The Chorus members have set themselves up as creators of song, but are overtaken by events. So too the audience must wonder how secure their own place in the scenario really is.

Iris and Lyssa

The madness of Heracles was an established mythological 'fact', but the direct involvement of Iris and Lyssa is yet another Euripidean innovation. We noted in Chapter 4 the likely appearance of Iris and Lyssa and their probable location on the roof of the house, linking them with the theme of architecture and safety in the play. Iris' opening words emphasise that they mean no harm to the city, but have come to attack the house of one man (824-5). Although the visual tableau may have the most immediate effect on the audience, the words Iris speaks are full of ambiguity. She notes as their target the man 'who, so people say, is the son of Zeus and Alcmene' (826), once again casting Heracles' ontological status into doubt.

The double epiphany of Iris and Lyssa allows Euripides to present an immediate portrait of divine conflict to contrast the Chorus' view of an overall divine plan. While Iris is untroubled by Hera's desire to punish Heracles, Lyssa, an individual character as much as a personification of madness,[4] questions the order, restating Heracles' merits, as Lee has discussed in his analysis of the scene.[5]

83

The description of the madness they will inflict is very violent, expressed in terms of driving an animal. Heracles will have 'gorgon-eyes', and be like 'a bull about to charge' (868-9). This is appropriate imagery for Lyssa, who is often portrayed as a hunter, and also complements the wider systems of imagery of sight and birds which we discussed in Chapter 4. Similarly, the nautical metaphors of ropes and seafaring which Lyssa uses are part of the theme of boats and yoking. A further strand comes from the description of the madness in serpentine form, which Slater has suggested is symbolic of the maternal hatred inspiring Hera's actions.[6] The madness is clearly intended as a perversion of Heracles' early glory. The man who tamed wild beasts is reduced to a bestial form, and his glory as victor is replaced with a 'crown of beautiful children, killed by his own hand' (839).[7]

Iris is straightforward in her determination to fulfil Hera's orders, and gives a clear statement about the purpose. Hera has long wished to attack Heracles, as Zeus' bastard son, but was unable to do so while he was pursuing the Labours. Now, at the first opportunity, she has attacked. This would be a simple version of the myth, as Hera's hatred of her husband's infidelity causes many disasters.[8] However, Iris' explanation raises as many questions as it answers, for her explanation of Hera's attack is phrased in legalistic language. She says that unless Heracles is punished, the gods will be nowhere and men will be great. This brings us to the central problem of the play, the nature of the madness and the question of responsibility and divine order.

Madness in tragedy

Divinely imposed madness is a frequent theme in Greek myth and in tragedy. Sometimes it is a direct punishment for a failure to respect a god, and the madness in such cases can cause an individual to kill a child. Agave in Euripides' *Bacchae* is driven mad for her failure to acknowledge Dionysus and kills her son Pentheus, mistaking him for a mountain lion. Aeschylus told the story of Lycurgus, who offends Dionysus; although we do

not know exactly how the story unfolded, later versions of the
myth make Lycurgus kill his son while mad, mistaking him for
a vine.[9] Madness can also be imposed to deflect an individual's
intention, as when Athena makes Ajax slaughter cows in place
of the Greek commanders at Troy.[10] There can also be forms of
madness which are not directly imposed, as when Orestes is
presented as hallucinating.[11]

Madness is not a straightforward phenomenon. Its relationship to normal psychology, illness and divine intervention
places it at the centre of a complex network of ideas about identity and the nature of the universe. Wide-ranging work on
madness in tragedy has been done by Padel, and we should
compare work on ancient medical ideas in tragedy by Collinge
and most recently Kosak on Euripides.[12] For our interpretation
of *Heracles*, the central problem is how far the madness is a
distortion of Heracles' basic behaviour or simply a misdirection.
When Agave kills Pentheus, her whole behaviour has been
changed, as when sane she would not have killed a mountain
lion, which is what she believes she is doing when she kills
Pentheus. However, in Sophocles' *Ajax* the madness which
Athena imposes is simply a misdirection. Ajax intended to kill
the Greeks, which is what he believes he is doing. Athena just
changes his perception, so that he sees cows as the Greeks. This
is a fundamental difference in the nature of madness, and our
assessment of the nature of Heracles' violence depends on the
type of madness Hera inflicts. Is he basically acting with his
normal behaviour (as Ajax),[13] or has his whole persona been
changed (as Agave)?

Heracles' symptoms – the messenger speech

The predictions from Lyssa and Iris are poetic, metaphorical,
suggesting that the nature of madness cannot be grasped in
words, and yet the description of Heracles given by the
Messenger is simple and physical (922ff.). The messenger
speech which describes the madness is full of details about the
onset of symptoms and the way Heracles reacts to those around
him (922ff.).

The setting at the altar, preparing for a sacrifice to give thanks for the defeat of Lycus, is initially a positive reframing of the opening scene of the play, but will be horribly perverted as the madness descends upon/enters into Heracles.[14] The first sign that something is wrong is noticed by the children, who turn to look at him, as he stands still and quiet (931). The madness first appears in Heracles' eyes which roll backwards and appear bloodshot (932-3), followed by foaming at the mouth (934). Bond notes that silence, rolling eyes and foaming at the mouth are symptoms of epilepsy, as described in the Hippocratic treatise 'The sacred disease', 7L.[15] Epilepsy was often described in the ancient and mediaeval world as 'The disease of Hercules' (*morbus Herculeus* in Latin), but that does not imply that Euripides thought of Heracles' madness in terms of an illness, only that he may have used current medical thinking to provide a persuasive description.[16] Other physical symptoms are noted by the Messenger (rolling head, groaning, strange laughter), but the main thrust of the madness appears to come at 936ff. when Heracles becomes confused about his surroundings.[17] Although Heracles still seems to recognise Amphitryon, addressing him at 936, he seems to see himself in different locations. This optical hallucination leads him to think he is in the house of Eurystheus, and he sets about killing 'Eurystheus' children'.

The assault of Hera appears first in the eyes and seems to consist mainly of an optical illusion, which fits well with the play's emphasis on issues of sight and perception.[18] Filhol has suggested that Heracles' violence stems from a problem with doubles, which links back to the problem of his double parentage.[19] In spite of the imposed madness, Heracles continues to exercise excellent motor skills, judging distance, and expressing his ideas in a forceful and articulate manner. This leads us to consider whether the madness is entirely one of misdirection.

Is it in his nature?

One of the central questions posed by the Messenger's description is whether the madness inflicted consisted solely of the optical distortion, or whether Heracles' behaviour was changed. That is to say, would Heracles have reacted in the same way if he had actually been faced by Eurystheus' small children, or is this violence a symptom of madness? Divine madness can take forms other than the simple optical. To take the *Bacchae* as an example, Pentheus comes under some sort of spell from Dionysus when he agrees to dress as a woman and claims to see 'two suns'. He becomes disorientated, and this madness causes him to act out of character. We might imagine that a similar form of madness could have been shown to afflict Heracles, so that he acted upon a violent impulse while still on one level acknowledging his wife and children.

Interpretation of this issue has provoked many conflicting readings of the play and Heracles' relative guilt. Hartigan has argued that Heracles is entirely innocent:

> His madness is not a sickness that grows from within, resulting from some crime or deed he has done, nor is it an aspect of his character which is just now with divine assistance being revealed. Herakles is destroyed by the jealous caprice of Hera and he in no way deserves it.[20]

Hartigan follows this with a strong assertion: 'Herakles in his madness is not doing a thing he would like to have done sane.'[21] This approach comes at one extreme of the critical spectrum, and is shared by Bond who sees the cause of the madness as simply the hostility of Hera.[22] Other readings suggest that Heracles is in some way implicated in the madness. However, there are many possible ways to configure the different elements. Bataille has argued that the madness was caused by resentment of Eurystheus,[23] and Burnett suggested that the madness was a punishment for the family's misdeeds, the hybris of abandoning hope and leaving the altar in response to Lycus' threats.[24] Wilamowitz originally suggested that the madness came from Heracles' megalomania, a view which he later disowned.[25] Kirk similarly suggests that the madness was within Heracles,[26] and Fitzgerald argues that child-killing is not uncharacteristic of Heracles as violent hero.[27]

A further line of interpretation has focused on the parallels between Lycus and Heracles. Krauss argues that Heracles and Lycus are very similar, and that the action of killing children is one which both men have in their nature.[28] The play sets up many links between the two figures, and this interpretation is persuasive, particularly when we consider the problematisation of Heracles' family role. The aftermath of the murders, which we will consider in Chapter 7, raises more questions. However, the interpretation of Heracles' actions is further complicated by Iris' statement that Heracles' must 'pay the penalty'. This introduces a problem about the relationship between Heracles and Hera.

Why does Hera attack him?

The attack of Hera is the opposite of the sort of divine reward which the Chorus had earlier discussed. Why does Heracles, the great benefactor, suffer this? One reason is simply the hatred of Hera. The animosity which Hera feels towards Heracles as Zeus' bastard son fits into a wider pattern of Hera's violent reactions to her husband's infidelities, such as her persecution of Io, or the engineered death of Semele, mother of Dionysus. It also conforms to Greek ideas about the traditional hostility of stepmothers to children.[29] This case, however, is more complicated, as suggested by the very name 'Heracles' (*Hera + Kleos* = 'Glory of Hera'). The dominant versions of Heracles' story tell of Hera's anger from his birth – in this play he briefly mentions how Hera sent snakes to kill him when he was newborn (1268-70). However, there is another strand of mythology which links Hera and Heracles more closely. This pattern has been explored in great depth by Slater, whose book *The Glory of Hera* sees the myth in terms of underlying psychological relationships between mothers and sons. A thorough discussion of this issue is beyond the scope of this book, but for the purposes of this discussion it is as well to note that this play does not focus on issues of motherhood, so it is unlikely that such material is directly relevant. We should, however, remember that there is a long history of animosity from Hera, so her decision to attack Heracles needs no direct explanation.[30] The only feature which needs comment is the timing, which Iris explains: Hera had been unable to attack Heracles while he was performing the Labours, but struck at the first available opportunity thereafter.

Gods in tragedy are capricious and easily provoked to violence as when Aphrodite attacks Hippolytus because he has not worshipped her, but Iris' explanation frames the debate in legalistic terms: Heracles must 'pay the penalty, or the gods will be nowhere' (841-2). The idea of paying a penalty or receiving justice has been seen earlier in the play, when the Chorus had spoken of Lycus receiving justice for his actions (756). There is, however, a key difference: Lycus receives justice for 'the things he has done', but Heracles' crime is not stated. Instead of referring to a past crime, the focus is on future consequences. His suffering is phrased as punishment necessary to avoid a cosmic catastrophe (840-2):

> He must be in no doubt about Hera's anger towards him, and my anger. The gods will be nothing, and mankind will be great if he does not pay the penalty.

On one level, this could be interpreted as an alternative expression of Hera's basic hatred, 'If I can't have my way, and destroy a mortal, then being a god is meaningless.' However, this does not explain the notion of 'paying a penalty'. The Greek phrasing is legalistic, the phrase *diken dounai*; in tragedy it is always used with reference to an action which has taken place within the scope of the play, or which the accusers allege has taken place. In this play, however, there is a conspicuous absence of explanation.

One of the most influential contributions to the debate has been Silk's contention that the crux of the play is Heracles' 'interstitial nature'.[31] Silk argues that Heracles has constantly challenged the limits of mortality, from his super-human snake-strangling strength as an infant to his capture of the golden apples of the Hesperides. The capture of Cerberus, the key Labour in this play which had delayed Heracles' arrival, is yet another example of his ability to go beyond the human realm. Silk argues that it is Heracles' very nature, his simple existence, which threatens to create the cosmic disharmony which Hera fears. The phrase 'pay the penalty' would then refer to a punishment not for anything which Heracles has *done* but for what he *is*. This interpretation is persuasive, though not without problems. It leaves unexplained why Hera should be in charge of righting cosmic wrongs, or why it should be acceptable for Heracles to continue with exactly the same 'interstitial nature' after the punishment has been inflicted. Interpretations of the play on similar lines have emphasised other aspects of the play, such as the capture of Cerberus, situating this act as the one boundary Heracles should not have crossed, and an act which deserved punishment which Hera was only too happy to provide.[32] Lee has suggested that the construction of the scene suggests that *dike* as a concept cannot be applied equally to human and divine spheres.[33] The least contentious reading of the play may be to say that the phrasing which Iris uses to explain Hera's actions may be deliberately ambiguous. This may be for internal reasons, such as Hera's wish to find a pretext for attacking Heracles, or it may be a device of the playwright's, appearing to give an explanation of the action, only to turn it into another source of confusion. At the end of the play Heracles questions whether we can truly comprehend the actions of the gods, so Euripides may be providing a deliberately paradoxical situation, where the audience must question even what they hear from the supposedly omniscient divine figures, as we will explore in the next chapter.

7

Suicide and the Gods

When Heracles comes round from his madness he finds himself bound like a shipwreck, a further development of the nautical imagery we discussed in the previous chapter. In one sense, this is an end to the action, but there is a final chapter to the story. Heracles' response to the disaster is to contemplate suicide, an impulse which is stalled by the arrival of Theseus. The play ends not with the realisation of disaster, but with an attempt to face the future. This section of the play builds on the issues, themes and problems raised in the earlier sections, and introduces new challenges for interpretation. Heracles' move towards suicide is linked with his rejection of the gods, and the 'solution', to go to Athens with Theseus, is by no means an uncomplicated one.

The aftermath

The Messenger concludes his account with a blunt assessment of Heracles' condition: 'I do not know of any mortal more wretched' (1014-15), and the Chorus members struggle to find a parallel for the disaster. They refer to the story of Procne, but she only killed one child, to Heracles' three. In a brief scene Amphitryon and the Chorus endeavour to come to terms with the tragedy. The tone is one of fear, as Amphitryon urges the Chorus not to wake Heracles, but the scene concludes with the Chorus' outrage at Zeus, as they cry out that he must hate his son. Although Heracles is initially disorientated, he quickly recovers his senses and realises what he has done. In response to his question 'Who did this?', Amphitryon replies 'You, your bow, and whichever of the gods is guilty' (1135). This is an example of over-determination, a common device in tragedy and Greek literature in general, whereby different levels of causation are seen to co-exist simultaneously. Heracles' first reaction is that he cannot continue to live (1146ff.), but his move towards death is forestalled by the arrival of Theseus. The next step in Heracles' thinking is a rejection of the gods (1255ff.). It includes an acceptance that the gods have rejected him, and develops into an existential angst, a questioning of the nature of the gods and their attitude towards mortals. Heracles rejects the traditional idea of reciprocity between gods and men.[1] The family's supplication was in vain, and now the sacrifice of thanks after the death of Lycus has been perverted, and the altar has been polluted.[2]

Suicide in tragedy

Garrison argues that suicide in tragedy normally functions to safeguard the values of the heroic society – death is preferable to a life of anguish and/or dishonour.[3] Suicide does not provoke the automatic condemnation which it receives within the Judeao-Christian tradition. Homeric heroes such as Odysseus and Achilles contemplate suicide as an option, but the picture in tragedy is more complicated. There is no single model of suicide, as every situation involves a cocktail of actions, reactions and different perspectives. In Sophocles' *Antigone* the suicide of Antigone herself is the alternative to a long-drawn out death by starvation, but it is also a defiant act, taking life and death into her own hands. Antigone's suicide is the matching action to her earlier decision, to defy authority and bury her brother Polyneices, knowing that such an act would be punished by death. Her suicide triggers the grief-driven suicide of Haemon, her intended bridegroom, and this in turn triggers the suicide of his mother, Eurydice. In each case the suicide is an immediate response to a situation, with little or no discussion. Heracles is different, not just because he rejects suicide, but because Euripides gives us an insight into the reasoning which accompanies the impulse. There are some parallels with situations featuring figures who are not true suicides, but who choose death with a conscious process, showing a similar reasoning to that which Heracles displays. These figures such as Menoiceus or Macaria volunteer to die in a situation where a death is called for, but they as individuals have not been named.[4] In both cases the motivation of 'glorious death rather than life with dishonour' is promoted as their reasoning. The closest parallels to Heracles' situation come from two plays, one in which the motivation is obvious but unspoken, and one in which the motivation is obvious but obscured.

In Sophocles' *Oedipus the King* Jocasta kills herself when the truth of Oedipus' situation is revealed. The motivation for her death is the wish to avoid the shame and pain of facing what she has done. Although unwitting, she has committed a terrible crime and in this respect her impulse to suicide parallels that of Heracles.

We should also note that in the same play Oedipus himself chooses self-mutilation through blinding rather than suicide – the implication is that he will not be able to face his family in death, suggesting that suicide is not simply the end of the story.

All the cases we have considered so far involve women and/or the young, which may suggest that suicide was not an option for adult male heroes. The second parallel case, however, comes from Sophocles' *Ajax*, and is explicitly framed as an issue of honour following an episode of madness, as we discussed in the previous chapter. When he recovers his senses Ajax is fixed in his resolve to die, and cannot be diverted from this course of action. His reasoning, however, is obscured by his attempts to misdirect others and to conceal his intentions. Unlike Heracles, whose opening wish is to die, Ajax conceals his true intent from those around him. The problem remains as to how would the original audience have responded to his suicide? Was it a noble act, or was it merely symptomatic of Ajax's wider failure to live within his own society? All of these cases show that, despite Garrison's arguments, the status of suicide is by no means clear cut. Although it can be a solution to a desperate situation, we should not assume that the Athenian audience would have accepted it uncritically as a good decision.

Within *Heracles* the debate arises early in the play. Megara presents herself as abiding by heroic codes of behaviour when she chose to leave the altar to secure an honourable death. In this respect her choice was not between life or death, but between two different forms of death. In that respect, their situation is closer to that of Polyxena in Euripides' *Hecuba*, who can choose only the manner of her death, but similarly chooses to uphold the value of honour. However, Megara is saved, and Heracles decides against suicide, so we are presented with a different set of questions. It would be easier to explain the dynamics which close the play if Heracles *had* killed himself, but the process of contemplating then rejecting suicide brings in a further aspect to the play. The murder of the children and Megara would be a powerful ending, capped by the final realisation of the disaster, a closure which would be paralleled with the *Bacchae* when Agave comes to her senses and realises that she has killed her son.

However, we then move into the final phase of the play where the suicide is rejected. Lines 1146-62 give a strong case for suicide, but the corresponding arguments against are not so neatly schematised. The arrival of Theseus distracts the focus from the immediate arguments, so that Heracles' decision to live on is part of a package of ideas rather than a simple victory of the Stronger over the Weaker argument. Heracles' decision is expressed in terms of bravery, and he decides that suicide would be cowardly, a view which modern audiences might well agree with. For an ancient audience, however, this position is not so obviously correct, and the play displays a discussion of the points at stake. His decision to reject suicide is connected to a range of issues. Yunis has argued that Heracles decides not to die because he realises that the gods have been unfair to him and comes to an 'awareness of shattered reciprocity with immoral gods'.[5] This places the emphasis on the gods, a view which draws some support from Theseus' own lines, as he assumes that Heracles' suicide is a threat against the gods. The majority of recent critics have argued in different ways that in rejecting suicide Heracles makes a positive choice to reject the accepted pattern of behaviour and find a new way of life. This leads some to discuss the wider issues at stake. De Romilly proposes that the scene is a piece of Euripidean provocation, suggesting that death is not the difficult option, but rather the easy one.[6] Garrison suggests that Heracles' decision shows him able 'to survive the transition from one set of ethics to another'.[7] The heroic world in which suicide would be appropriate has been shown to be problematic and compromised, and so Heracles' rejection of suicide is in fact a rejection of the whole value system on which his earlier actions had been based.

Fitzgerald argues that 'cowardice is a formalised subject of the play' and suggests that the rejection of suicide is only one move in the final scenes, an indication of the paradox which Heracles cannot solve:[8] either he rejects the entire basis of his previous physical heroism, or he takes up the weapons which have previously defined him and resumes his old role, which essentially is an act of cowardice as it denies the truth. Thus, there is a conflict at the end of the play when Heracles appears to reject the gods and the old beliefs about strength etc, but still takes up the old weapons.

The 'message' of the play, then, may be that inexplicable tragedies may befall even the best of men, and that divine protection is no protection and no comfort. This reading would emphasise the mortal aspects of Heracles' character, and the universal relevance of the story to audiences ancient and modern. Heracles' final response may be seen as a call to face life and struggle on with the help of friends, no matter what may befall you. Such attitudes would probably be called 'heroic' by modern audiences, and could prefigure the role of Heracles as a figurehead for Stoic philosophy, which we will consider in the final chapter.

Rejecting the gods

To turn away from divine protection and put your faith in friends is a viewpoint deceptively familiar to modern audiences who have experience of humanistic philosophies. For a fifth-century audience, however, this would be far more controversial. The gods were a focus of everyday life, from the rituals of birth and death to political life and warfare. Ignoring the gods was not an option, but the traditional processes of supplication and sacrifice have been perverted. It is significant that Heracles' final words value friendship over 'wealth and strength', so the contrast is not between divine and mortal support but between different types of mortal support. When Heracles recognises what he has done he expresses doubts about the very nature of the gods. He argues that Hera does not deserve to be worshipped, and questions whether the gods known through art and literature are really gods, calling popular mythology 'the wretched stories of poets' (1346). This speculation would have been recognisable to some of the original audience. The idea that mortal stories do not reflect real divinity was suggested by the early philosopher Xenophanes.[9] This hint of philosophical sophistication is typically Euripidean, but it is not followed to its conclusion by Heracles the character. As he accepts Theseus' offer of help, he implicitly accepts that his own position is not tenable. We must wonder why Euripides included these sentiments. Two reasons are particularly plausible. Firstly, they indicate the extent to which Heracles has fallen low, and suggest that *in extremis* divinity is no help. Similarly, at the end of Euripides' *Hippolytus* the respect of Artemis is cold comfort for Hippolytus and his family. Recent criticism has often suggested that the play's manipulation of ideas of divinity is designed to show the impossibility of grasping cosmic concepts. Papadopoulou has argued that the gap between humans and gods is shown to be unbridgeable, and Lawrence has argued that Heracles struggles to re-orientate himself in a secular world, without the gods.[10]

Another reason for the inclusion of this philosophical speculation is connected to the process of tragedy itself. We have earlier heard the Chorus struggle to find a mythological parallel for Heracles' suffering, questioning the value of stories for human situations. Now with the repeated idea that the stories of poets may not reflect the reality of divinity, Euripides is directly questioning the status *of this very play*. If we cannot trust the words of poets, how should we interpret this poetic offering? Furthermore, if the poets know nothing about the gods, how should we understand the appearance of Iris and Lyssa in the play? They seem to give an explanation for the events that unfold, but is there any reason to believe them? The end of the play makes the audience re-evaluate their experience of watching the drama, like a cat chasing its tail. Heracles' cries of pain are not merely the random outpourings of a grief-stricken man.

In other plays Euripides raises similar questions about the nature of storytelling and tragedy. We may think of Euripides' *Electra* where Electra pours scorn on the conventions of Aeschylean theatre, dismissing them as the trickery of theatre, while still performing an act of theatre.[11] In Euripides' *Bacchae* we see an illusion within the dramatic illusion as the text suggests an earthquake which may all be a collective hallucination. It may be that Euripides was employing a similar device in the *Heracles*, and that the final scenes are designed to make us uncertain of what we have just 'witnessed'. Are we, like Megara's children, simply told stories to distract us? In the course of watching the play can we remember exactly what Iris said? Did we 'see' Iris and Lyssa in the same way in which Heracles 'saw' the children of Eurystheus? The play leaves us with no answers, just a sense that something is wrong. This lack of closure is one of the reasons which have led some critics to condemn the structure of the play. It may be, however, that Euripides was *trying* to upset his audience, and that the failure of generations of scholars to 'solve' the play is simply a mark of his success.

Zeus and Athena

If the on-stage appearance of Iris and Lyssa is paradoxical, what should we make of Athena's intervention in the madness, and how should we interpret the role of Zeus in the play? 'Where is Zeus?' is a question posed by several characters. Zeus does not directly intervene to save the family from Lycus' attack, nor does he prevent that of Hera. We are not told that he sent Athena to save Amphitryon, and he sends no word to Heracles at the end. Even if he was unable to intervene to stop Hera, we might have expected some expression of his regard after the event. In one sense, this is the familiar Zeus of Greek tragedy, distant, disengaged, an overall idea of divinity, rather than an individualised god. This is the vague, background idea of Zeus which we see in Aeschylus' *Agamemnon*, referred to as 'Zeus, whoever he may be', rather than the young, active tyrant behind the scenes of *Prometheus Bound*.[12]

However, in the *Heracles* there is reason why Zeus might be expected to be involved, as father of Heracles. Amphitryon certainly thinks he should intervene. The question then takes us back to the discussion of fatherhood which we looked at in Chapter 5. In Greek myth Zeus is not traditionally a hands-on father. His greatest involvement with the children he fathers on mortal women comes after their death. The episode in Homer's *Iliad* Book 16.433ff. gives us a good example of this situation. Zeus sees that his son Sarpedon is fated to die, and contemplates saving him. Hera remonstrates that such an act would be wrong, and so Zeus allows Sarpedon to die, but then sends Sleep and Death to rescue his body. Zeus' role as father of the gods gives him responsibilities which take precedence over what might be termed 'normal' family responsibilities. It may be that this is also the situation which ultimately pertains to Heracles, and that for all Zeus' desire to engage with his family he cannot escape from the more powerful forces to which his role ties him. So, while the distant role of Zeus can be explained in traditional mythological terms, it is also appropriate to the play's discussion of the nature of fatherhood and the conflict between public and private responsibilities.

The arrival of Athena is described by the Messenger as an intervention to stop Heracles committing parricide. This is a plausible explanation, but her role remains ill-defined. While she may be acting as an agent of Zeus, she may also be acting as Heracles' protector,[13] or because of a general concern for the rights of fathers.[14] Athena has a complicated set of roles in Greek religion, as she is the one who imposes the madness on Ajax.[15] There are also links between Athena and Zeus and Heracles which suggest a close relationship.[16] However, her role as patron goddess of Athens gives the episode a more immediate link to the original audience, and connects her with Theseus, who arrives shortly afterwards.[17] As Athena stops the physical harm, Theseus provides a solution to the emotional chaos which ensues, as we will discuss in the following chapter.

8

Theseus and the Role of Friendship

Greek tragedy often ends with the central character facing his disaster, so the ending of *Heracles* is made all the more complex by the arrival of Theseus, and his role in changing the direction of Heracles' thoughts. Some critics have downplayed Theseus' importance, seeing the decisive changes coming from Heracles' own thinking, but for many critics the arrival of Theseus is a pivotal feature of the story. It is difficult to judge the contribution which Theseus makes to the resolution. He offers physical help, but does he actually help Heracles with his pain? Does Heracles' accept Theseus' arguments, and the view of the gods Theseus proposes? Should we take Theseus' view as representing the likely views of the original audience? Theseus' intervention is within the framework of 'friendship' rather than philosphical argumentation, and Heracles himself turns away from his philosophical approach to conclude the play with the gnomic assertion, 'Any man who wishes to have money or strength rather than good friends is out of his mind' (1425-6). Is this then a simple outcome, that friendship conquers all? The interpretation of this point is central to an understanding of the play as a whole, and there is no scholarly consensus.

Friendship and reciprocity

The value of friendship is referred to at several points in the play. In his opening speech, Amphitryon notes the limitations to friendship:

> As for friends, some I see are not to be relied upon, while those
>   deserving of the name

are powerless to assist. So it is when men encounter misfortune.
  I pray that no friend
of mine, even a mere acquaintance, may have this experience;
  there is no surer test of friendship.[1]

He outlines Heracles' good deeds, and says that Greece in
return should care for his children (217ff.) When Heracles
returns to save the family he is astonished that no one has
helped them before, but Megara replies 'Bad luck has no
friends' (561). Salvation comes from Heracles alone, not from
'Zeus the Saviour', or from human friends. This would suggest
that the only support comes from family, but after the murders
the family structure is in tatters. When Heracles awakes from
his madness he has nothing to draw upon. His physical strength
is worse than useless, his father is helpless and the gods have
either attacked him, or offered at best limited help against
attack. Where, then, can he turn for help?

The answer comes in the form of Theseus, a representative
of the possibility of human friendship and a social structure
within the religious life of Athens. Divine friendship is unreli-
able, as it relies on unseen forces and involves an unequal
distribution of power, rather than any idea of reciprocity. By
contrast, friendship between men can be demonstrated and
developed so that it proves a reliable source of support, even
though it failed the family in the face of Lycus' threat. Just as
Heracles turns away from his divine heritage, and asserts the
priority of Amphitryon's claim to fatherhood (see Chapter 5), so
he turns away from divine support, or features which could be
considered 'divinely given', and looks instead to the stability of
human friendship. Heracles knows where he stands with
Theseus. As he had offered help to Theseus in Hades, Theseus
repays this to support him in his time of need; Heracles brought
Theseus out of Hades, and Theseus takes Heracles to Athens.

The structural parallels are clear, but the extent of this
friendship is open to interpretation. The pragmatic aspects of
friendship were very prominent in the Greek traditions.
Aristotle distinguished between three different types of friendships, that based on good character, and those grounded in

pleasure or usefulness.[2] Millett emphasises the utility of friends and the importance of reciprocal arrangements in Greek society,[3] whereas Konstan goes further, stressing the importance of decency and right feeling.[4] In tragedy, friendship and its place in society are at issue in several plays. A similar statement to Heracles' occurs in Euripides' *Orestes*, where the close comradeship between Orestes and Pylades is emphasised.[5] At the end of *Heracles* Konstan sees Theseus as a true friend, arguing that it is not just Theseus' actions which are correct, as he shares Heracles' pain (1202), and is not afraid of incurring pollution.[6] We should also note that Theseus too shares a double parentage, as child of Aegeus/Poseidon, so he has some claim to understand the cosmic dilemma Heracles faces.[7]

The importance of the idea of reciprocal friendship increases, if we accept that *Heracles* was part of a connected trilogy. Dobrov follows Mette in suggesting that *Heracles* came after *Peirithous*, so that the audience had seen the previous act of friendship which Theseus repays.[8] The personal relationship between the two characters is emphasised, but there are wider political and religious links for the original audience. Theseus offers Heracles the friendship of the entire city of Athens (1331-3), providing an aetiology for the centrality of Heracles in Athens in the fifth century.[9] This leads us to consider the social and political aspects of friendship.

Political friendship

The bond of *philia* between Herakles and Theseus was amplified in Euripides' play into a vivid cultural reciprocity. Herakles was aggressively assimilated into Athens while the juxtaposition of Theseus and Herakles highlighted the latter's well-known status as the paradigm for Theseus' ever-evolving heroic 'career'.

Dobrov, *Figures of Play*, p. 146

By the fifth century Theseus had been enthusiastically adopted as the great hero of Athens. As Athens grew in strength as a Mediterranean power from the late sixth century onwards, there were concerted efforts to increase the profile of Theseus, often by modelling his story on the more famous, pan-Hellenic stories of Heracles. So Theseus became credited with his own series of labours, as can be seen on the sculptures of the Athenian Temple of Hephaestus and Athena. This temple, built in the Doric style starting around 449 BCE, is one of the most well-preserved monuments of classical Athens, and was until comparatively recently known as the Theseion, because of the prominence of scenes showing Theseus' exploits.[10] The temple is in the heart of Athens, at the western edge of the Agora, the central marketplace of Athens, and so would have given the hero a conspicuous presence in the city. The arrival of Theseus in *Heracles* comes as the benign counterpart to the arrival of Lyssa and Iris, and allies Theseus with Athena, who saves Amphitryon. He offers friendship, a place of refuge for a suppliant and behaves in a generous manner. All these qualities could be taken as positive reflections of the ideal Athenian self-image. Theseus is no longer in the shadow of Heracles, he is able to save him through his intellectual and moral character. Furthermore, Hall has argued that the play shows the Athenian appropriation of Heracles.[11] While the end of the play leaves a number of issues unresolved for modern audiences, the original audience may have believed it a satisfying ending if judged from an Athenocentric position. That is to say, if they believed that Theseus' actions were entirely honourable, the story could have been understood as a panegyric of Athenian power and policy.

Certainly the role of Theseus in some plays can be seen as positive, as in Euripides' *Suppliants* where he intervenes with great diplomacy to solve a crisis, or in Sophocles' *Oedipus at Colonus* when Theseus offers asylum to Oedipus.[12] The act of offering refuge, as Theseus does to Heracles, was an important element of Athenian self-presentation, a political pattern referred to positively in a number of contexts, as well discussed by Loraux.[13] We may consider the fact that a playwright in competition at the *City Dionysia* had a vested interest in flattering his audience, and the judges might respond well to a portrayal of their national hero in a positive light, Theseus saving the great hero Heracles.

Friendship in a wider context can also be read as a positive comment as a political principle of the Athenian democracy, promoting friendship among equals both inside the democracy and in relations with other states. Konstan has noted the importance of *philia* in inter-state relations as a source of support and communication additional to *xenia*, the protocols of hospitality protected by Zeus.[14] To extrapolate from this position, the democracy can be viewed as an extension of the principle of reciprocal friendship, establishing sound bonds between individuals and society. This form of interconnection is a humanistic response to a situation when there appears to be no reciprocity between men and gods, the situation which Heracles seems to face.

Thus we can construct a broadly positive reading of the play which ends on a positive note, so the Athenians may have gone away feeling proud of their city and justified in their promotion of friendship. Burnett suggests that the play allows the audience to enjoy a sense of anticipated glory as Heracles takes his place in Athens, and Foley proposes that a process of civic integration is the assumed conclusion of the story once Heracles leaves with Theseus.[15] However, if we refer back to Aristotle's enumeration of the three types of friendship, we may question whether Theseus' friendship really is a true friendship, based on moral virtue, and this calls into doubt the entire ending of the play.

Problematic friendship

If we return to the statement which some have taken as programmatic, 'Value nothing more than friends', there are details of the structure and placement which raise uncomfortable issues. The key phrase comes immediately after Heracles has used the *epholkis* image for the second time, casting himself as the small boat to Theseus' ship (as discussed in Chapter 4). Heracles followed the first use of the image with the gnomic 'All mankind love their children', but that assertion is called into question by his subsequent actions, killing the 'children of Eurystheus'. At the end of the play the same structure is used, *epholkis* image followed by a gnomic statement, so we may wonder whether the second assertion is any less problematic than the first.

If Heracles may not be an ideal judge of philosophical issues, maybe his particular friendship with Theseus is not a model we should accept uncritically. The act of friendship which Theseus accomplishes is formally satisfying, as it gives Heracles a place to stay. However, some critics have questioned whether Theseus as an individual engages with Heracles so as to change his mind about the suicide, which as we noted is a debate about cowardice. Michelini has argued that Theseus engages only on a superficial level.[16] Even Heracles seems to think that there is not a true reciprocity between himself and Theseus, as he asserts the value of his former deeds.[17] So, if the friendship Theseus offers is open to question, what of the earlier action? Is the friendship between Theseus and Heracles really an exemplar for human interaction? Is Theseus the sort of man you want as your friend?

Whether or not the *Peirithous* was part of the trilogy, the Athenian audience would have known why Theseus was in Hades – he was helping his friend; so far so good. However, the reason why Peirithous was in Hades was to abduct Persephone – not so good. We may question whether Theseus should have been helping Peirithous, and whether Heracles should have helped them both. Is this a friendship based on moral rectitude in an Aristotelian model? This detail could perhaps be dismissed if it were an isolated incident, but unfortunately the myth of Theseus is filled with episodes which reflect badly on his character. There are two other abductions, to start with, the abduction of Helen and of the Amazon queen Hippolyte.[18] Theseus shows no sense of reciprocal loyalty towards Ariadne who helps him kill the Minotaur, as he abandons her on Naxos.[19] On returning from Naxos Theseus causes the death of his father Aegeus because he forgets to change the colour of his sails – the old man sees the black sails signalling failure and kills himself.[20] The myth indicates what today we would categorise as an attitude problem.

What then are we to make of this figure, the great civic hero at the centre of national identity whose life story contained so many incidents where his behaviour was questionable? Mills has argued that the Athenians were able to be creative in their attitude towards the hero, and to focus on his positive attributes.[21] However, Walker has analysed the roles which Theseus played in the Athenian imagination, and argued that there were real concerns, not just about the mythological figure, but about the wider situation for which he was a figurehead:[22] as the Athenians developed an empire, which brought great wealth, but demanded a number of political and moral compromises, it seems that there was an increasing feeling of unease among some in Athens about the way the city was progressing. Given that the figure of Theseus could be seen as problematic in the fifth century, there are a number of potential problems about his role in *Heracles*. While Heracles presents a simple, positive view of friendship, the original audience may well have been aware that friendship was not a simple matter. Helping friends was good, but what should you do when such an act compromised your own position or your moral code? The value which Heracles placed on Theseus' friendship could be seen as detrimental to his family commitments, causing him to expose them to Lycus and to leave his father at the end of the play; and what sort of man was Theseus to inspire such loyalty? For Aristotle, the philosophical view was clear; a friend who was not morally upright was not a real friend and thus the reciprocal obligations of friendship did not apply. We must, therefore, question whether the lauded friendship in this play is really the model of good conduct which it claims to be. Another reason to question the value of friendship comes from the other great Euripidean partnership, that between Orestes and Pylades, a friendship which inspires the assertion quoted above. In that play, however, the character of Orestes is of doubtful moral quality, and we must wonder whether the Athenian audience would have valued this friendship highly.[23]

A more negative view of the friendship is proposed by Dunn who notes that Theseus is not a successful *deus ex machina*, that Heracles is consistently reluctant to accept Theseus' offer, and that when they leave there is no real force in it.

By the time they leave the stage a few lines later [after 1413], Theseus' magnanimous gesture has been emptied of all authority, and reduced to the bickering among friends.[24]

Athenian disquiet?

If the personal level of interaction is problematic, what then of the wider implications? The supreme act of friendship offered by Theseus, to take in a man who has killed his children and give him a place of honour in Athens, could be very uncomfortable for the original audience. Theseus is the Athenian king, and although he offers friendship on a personal level, his offer of help implies the acquiescence of the people of Athens in the mythical past and, by extension, in contemporary fifth-century Athens as well, although Dunn stresses that Theseus is a private citizen.[25]

While the offers of sanctuary in Euripides' *Suppliants* and *Children of Heracles*, and Sophocles' *Oedipus at Colonus*, are presented in generally positive light, there is a more direct comparison which is far less likely to provoke feelings of patriotic pride. In Euripides' *Medea* the end of the play comes as Medea has killed her children and flees to Athens after she has secured the offer of a place of refuge from King Aegeus (father of Theseus). This offer of sanctuary had a reciprocal element, as Medea had promised to cure Aegeus of his infertility. Although he is aware that Medea is planning to take revenge on her husband, Aegeus is not told that the children are to be killed; but the oath that he swears nevertheless commits him to take in Medea whatever happens. Sfyroeras has discussed this scene in some detail, arguing that the arrival of Aegeus draws the audience more deeply into the plot, with Aegeus as a 'surrogate audience member' making all Athens, mythological and present day, complicit in Medea's plot.[26] It is the promised support of Athens which allows Medea the opportunity to take revenge by killing the children. Sfyroeras argues persuasively that the unwitting support which Aegeus gives to Medea's crime would have been uncomfortable viewing for the Athenian audience.

The anxiety over Athens' role as accessory to Medea's infanticide is reinforced by the chorus of Corinthian women who sing a long ode praising Athens as a city of beauty and culture. They conclude by asking Medea 'How can such a city give you refuge?' (Euripides' *Medea*, vv. 846ff.). And yet, in some versions, the next stage of the myth indicates the danger posed to Athens where Medea plots the death of the young Theseus. Thus, in the stories of Medea and Heracles Athens is shown as a place which will welcome those who have committed the terrible crime of infanticide. The link between the two figures was made in certain ancient contexts: there is a version of the myth in which Medea is actually the one who cures Heracles of his madness, and there is a vase which shows the two of them at Eleusis.[27] The two crimes are not identical, for, unlike Medea's, Heracles' crime was unwitting. Nevertheless, blood pollution in Greek religion attached itself even to accidental homicides.[28] Theseus makes it clear that he is welcoming Heracles on behalf of Athens, and that this act will reflect on all Athenians (1331-2): 'After your death, the entire city of Athens will honour you.' The fifth-century audience, therefore, were invited to question whether this association is really appropriate. The relationship between myth and contemporary fifth-century Athenian society is held up to scrutiny in this play, and the original audience may well have been left with a sense of unease, not only about the metaphysical questions, but also about their own identity as Athenians. The role of Theseus is not, however, the only aspect of the play which deserves consideration in a specifically Athenian context. The issue of political friendship may also be more complicated than it at first appears.

The dark side of Athenian political friendship

Attempts to link particular tragedies to specific events in Athenian history are problematic even when we know the date of the original production. The timing of the *City Dionysia* festival meant that the plays could air political ideas just as the new political and military season was starting. While it is undoubtedly true that contemporary issues were reflected in the plays, the timing could seldom have been precise, not least because the effort to write and produce a series of plays for a given year must have started months before each festival. Any political debate which was taken as a topical focus when writing a play may well have been overtaken by events by the time the play was staged. Returning to an old issue would not have been a wise strategy for dramatists who were in competition with each other. There are very few surviving tragedies where a strong link can be drawn between contemporary events and the myth, the one notable exception being Aeschylus' *Oresteia* trilogy of 458 BCE which reflects political developments some three years earlier.

In general, it is fair to say that the Greek tragedians responded to issues and themes in political life rather than particular incidents or policies. We should never forget that the plays were interacting with literary and philosophical debates as well as political ones, and that the very strength of Greek myth lay in its ability to comment on widely felt concerns without direct references. The *Heracles* is one of the plays for which we do not know the date of original performance, but expert opinion is generally agreed that it is likely to have been between 420 and 416 BCE.[29] This places it during a crucial period in the Peloponnesian War, which Athens and her allies fought against the Peloponnesians, led by Sparta. The war was a long-running affair, starting around 431 BCE, with a brief cessation in 421, and continuing until 404 when Athens was defeated. Throughout the progress of the war the two sides were evenly matched, with conflict in a number of areas in the Mediterranean. Athens itself was besieged for many years, with the Spartans camped in Attica, making the citizens reliant on the navy to support them. Warfare was, therefore, a constant preoccupation of Athens during this period. What effect should knowledge of this historical context have on our understanding of *Heracles*?

The issue of friendship may have had topical relevance, in a wider national context. Athens' relationship with her allies was increasingly precarious as the war progressed, mainly because the allies were in the most part subject states of the Athenian empire, providing Athens with a yearly tribute payment.

Heracles' belief that you should stick with your friends even in the darkest of hours could be read as a comment on the need for Athens to support her allies. Indeed, the idea of wider friendship links within Greece is raised in the play from Amphitryon's charge that all of Greece stands accused of cowardice for not protecting Heracles' family and repaying the debts they owe to him (220ff.). Unfortunately, as we have discussed above, if this is a theme for Athenian audiences there is a darker side to it, compelling the Athenians to contemplate the nature of their friendships, the demands they make on their friends, and the risks they run in supporting them. Does Athens show support of her friends commensurate with the demands she makes on them? If human friendship is the only basis for society, is Athens respecting this reciprocity?

To start with, although Athenian democracy emphasised human interaction, it was by no means dismissive of reciprocity with the gods. Certainly the gods could be difficult to understand, but the basic practices of Greek religion assumed a two-way process – worship for the gods procured support for mortals. Athens' rise to power in the fifth century was often represented in terms of divine pleasure and the support of the gods, particularly the support of Athena. Heracles might have had reason to doubt the protection of the gods, but Athenians might well have greater confidence in their own position. While an individual might not compare himself to the great figure of Heracles, the ideology of democracy placed individuals within the context of the state, and perhaps the state of Athens as a whole could have a stronger claim on a reciprocal relationship with the gods.

The meaning of life

If the apparent simplicity of Heracles' final words is deceptive, what then do we make of the end of the play? One solution may be to consider further the issue of divine purpose and humanist responses which we noted in the previous chapter. Towards the end of the century thinkers such as Socrates and his pupil Plato were proposing ideas about the universe which stressed the need to analyse life through dialogue with others. Plato's dialogue the *Ion* casts a critical eye over the 'stories of poets' which Euripides holds up to scrutiny in *Heracles*. In general terms, Euripidean drama shows some sympathy with philosophical speculations of the period, but in this play we may see a figure who gets it wrong. Heracles raises his doubts about the gods, but his partner in the dialogue is Theseus, who does not engage with the debate, but offers him physical support. Not only are Heracles' theological doubts not resolved, there is not even any discussion of them. The play may be viewed as deliberately aporetic, offering an impasse, but no solution, an idea proposed in different ways by a number of critics: Lee suggests that *dike*, justice, cannot be equally applied to human and divine spheres;[30] Papadopoulou argues that the gulf between humans and gods is unbridgeable;[31] Rehm suggests that the end of the play and the absence of the Chorus imply an ultimate failure of the artistic project – there are no words to live up to what Hera has done.[32] These readings speak to modern audiences, who often find the end of the play unsatisfying, but what of the ancient audience?

The Chorus often has the last word in tragedy, providing some clues to the central idea of the play, but the ending of this story lacks this form of structural closure. The emotional state of the original audience may involve horror at what Heracles has suffered, combined with some sense of relief that there is some resolution, and civic pride that their hero, Theseus, has offered support to Heracles. It is difficult to assess the extent to which the intellectual and theological problems of the play impinge on the broader emotional tone at the end. Would members of the original audience have felt satisfied, or would they have turned to each other in a state of confusion, unsure of what they had witnessed? It would be interesting if we could study the satyr play which Euripides presented after *Heracles* to see whether he had any strategy for modulating the audience's response to the story of the great fallen hero. As we cannot adequately judge the emotional state of individual audience members, we can only think about the immediate physical and political surroundings of the original Athenian audience.

If the issue of friendship may touch upon international concerns, then the depiction of family relationships has resonance for the domestic situation of Athens. The tableau which opens the play, a family without its adult male figure, consisting of the old, the young and the women, would have been one which was familiar in contemporary Athens when many of the adult males were fighting away from home for long periods of time. The traditional structures of the *oikos* were coming under strain, with the traditional relationships between old and young, men and women changing in response to new situations.[33] Greek literature had from its earliest beginnings acknowledged the problem facing men in times of war: protect your family at home or leave them to fight for their protection in the world at large, a situation shown by the presence of the Trojan families in Homer's *Iliad*. This situation may have become increasingly pressing for Athenian society.

Furthermore, the emphasis with which Euripides tells Heracles' story may suggest two other issues. Firstly, that prolonged exposure to warfare may have brought undesirable elements into Athenian domestic society, such as increased avarice and a desire for individual glory. This is the idea which Thucydides focuses on in his account of the debate before the Sicilian expedition, when Nicias accuses Alcibiades of favouring the expedition for selfish ends.[34] This debate, set in 415 BCE, indicates that the social and political climate in Athens was changing during the period. A second related idea may be that there had been a growth in individualism at the expense of family loyalty and responsibility. Heracles is shown as having a spectacular public profile, a role in the world which focuses on his *individual* strengths, rather than placing him in a family context. We see from the start of the play that Heracles' family history is ambiguous, denying him the framework of family status which was traditionally the baseline for individual glory. Furthermore, the idea of immortality in Greek culture was strongly tied to the idea of having children, who would continue your name and tend the family cults. For Heracles, his immortality comes from his individual exploits and the friendship offered by Theseus, but it comes at the expense of his family

112

life, what we might term his 'mortal immortality'. Fifth-century Athenians were not generally imbued with mythological super-strength, but there was an increasing move towards individualism.[35] This was seen in the rise of philosophy, and the idea that the individual had a responsibility for his own destiny. Even the idea of loyalty to one's city-state as a defining feature of an individual's identity was under threat. This change is exemplified by the history of Alcibiades who, as we mentioned earlier, was charged with selfish aims. As the war progressed Alcibiades abandoned his loyalty to Athens, moving over to the Spartan side, and eventually collaborating with the Persians. In such a climate, the story of Heracles could have been taken as a warning to value family structures, rather than pursue individual aims and friendships.

9

After Euripides

The opening chapters of this volume explored the broad sweep of mythology which underlies the play. Euripides' account must be read as just one instantiation of just one part of the myth of Heracles, which itself is connected to a range of other stories in the overarching framework of Greek mythology and religion. It is, therefore, not surprising that the reception history of the play is only a small part of the reception history of all the Heracles myths, and cannot be studied in isolation. As a thorough survey of Heracles' role after the fifth century is impossible to include in a book of this nature, this chapter will instead concentrate on two specific questions. What, if anything, does the play have to say to modern audiences? How have changing fashions and interpretations of Heracles brought us to this point? The discussion will be divided into three sections, beginning with the first stage of reception, the transformation which saw the Greek Heracles merge with, and/or develop into, the Roman Hercules. We will then examine the major trends in the reception of Heracles/Hercules to the twentieth century. That section of material is well covered by Galinsky,[1] so I will note particular points of interest for the reception of Euripides' play, rather than attempting to give an detailed overview. To conclude, we will consider the place of Heracles the character and *Heracles* the play in the twentieth and twenty-first centuries.

The first stage of reception

By the end of the fifth century Heracles was a figure known in a number of guises, from the philosophical exemplar to the drunken, violent stock figure of comedy. The immediate impetus for the survival of Euripides' play is likely to have been the wider popularity of tragedy in the Greek colonies of Italy, the area commonly referred to as *Magna Graecia* or *Megalê Hellas* (Great Greece).[2] The importation of tragedy may have been a way for the disparate Greek communities to demonstrate their pride in their national identity. Stories about Heracles also had a place in Magna Graecia, for ideas of genealogy still linked these Greek communities to their ancestral myths, some of which claimed Heracles as the mythical founder of the family line. The popularity of theatre in this part of the world has left us our most useful source of visual evidence about ancient tragedy, as surviving vases showing theatrical scenes are far more numerous from fourth-century Italy than from fifth-century Athens.[3] The only surviving explicit visual image of the madness of Heracles comes from this period, from a Red-Figure Paestan calyx-krater.[4] The scene shows Heracles with a child in his arms, on the point of throwing the child into a burning pile of furniture. Megara is depicted to one side, and Alcmene and Iolaus are shown looking on from above. Also depicted is Mania (madness) holding a whip. The scene does not directly correspond to Euripides' presentation, in the cast and the manner of the killing, but the image may have been influenced by theatrical presentations of the story.[5] The act of throwing the child into a fire may be an early variant or the original means of death, for it is mythologically appropriate. It is a reversal of the motif by which individuals can transcend their mortality, as Heracles himself does when he is deified after his death on a pyre at Oeta. Children can be made immortal through this method, but the reverse process can also occur, as when Meleager is killed by a fire brand through the use of sympathetic magic. In Heracles' life, the motif of burning his children would be a further reference to the problem of mortality and immortality which is central to this plot.[6] We can see even at this early stage that there was a process of reception which was reacting to, and re-interpreting, accounts of the madness. Although we have studied *Heracles* as a product of Athenian enterprise, the myth had far wider currency, and the reception history of the play takes on a far greater geographical compass.[7]

The Hellenistic world

After the Athenians were defeated in the Peloponnesian War at the end of the fifth century the city never regained its dominant position as a Mediterranean superpower, despite rapid political recrudescence and a continued cultural development with the growth of oratory and philosophy. The next grand expansion in the Greek world came from Macedon, first under the rule of Philip II, and then under his son, Alexander the Great. Before dying at the age of thirty-two in 323 BCE, Alexander established himself as the ruler of the Greek states, most of the Mediterranean communities, the old Persian empire and much of central Asia. In his own time Alexander was likened to Heracles, an act of political propaganda which would come to inspire the use of Heracles in the Roman empire. Alexander himself may have explicitly claimed to be his direct descendant.[8] He was said to have dressed in lion skins, and was shown on Macedonian coins posing as Heracles.[9] Although his empire was soon fragmented after his death, the cultural legacy of the expansion survived and flourished due to the founding of Alexandria. This city, founded in 331 BCE in Egypt, became a centre for scholarship and the arts. The site of an old village, it became the main port of Egypt, with a strategically important position north-west of the Nile delta. A cosmopolitan city, mixing Greek with Egyptian, Jewish and other Eastern traditions, it provided one of the strongest links between Greek culture and the growing power of Rome.

The Hellenistic period (the term given to the years from the death of Alexander in 323 to the death of Cleopatra VII of Egypt in 30 BCE) saw the rise of Alexandria as an artistic and intellectual focus, and from this period survive a number of works which indicate how the figure of Heracles was re-imagined for new audiences. In sculpture, Heracles could be portrayed either as the athletic, muscular god of the gymnasium or as the leaning figure heavy with mortal worries, and there were a number of

Hellenistic dramas entitled 'Heracles'.[10] In Apollonius Rhodius' epic poem *Argonautica* Heracles is the great strong man, over-whelmed by his passions, who abandons the expedition to search for his lover, Hylas. This particular emphasis relates to increased interest in the Hellenistic period in the portrayal of emotional states centred on the individual which could transcend national boundaries. Heracles was fast becoming an international hero, taking on new forms but still retaining key features which would have been familiar to the audiences of fifth-century Athens. We have no direct information about how this one Euripidean play was received, but the tragedies as a body of work were being edited, studied and copied throughout the period. The first collection of Euripides' plays was assembled by Dicaerclius and Callimachus in the early third century, although 'official' copies of plays were first created in fourth-century Lycurgan Athens. Philochorus (*c.* 306-260 BCE) wrote a treatise on the mythology of Euripides' plays, and they continued to influence the literary tradition, as writers such as Apollonius looked back to tragedy for reference points as they developed their own examinations of emotional and psychological states. The theme of madness was also a subject of interest in medical circles, with the development of writings following the Hippocratic traditions.[11] In such a climate, the play would have survived through a number of routes.

The Roman world

When the Romans conquered the Greek cities in the third and second centuries BCE, Roman religion was transformed by contact with Greek culture, and the mythology of the two polytheistic religions merged to form what we today refer to as Graeco-Roman myth. Some figures from Greek myth adopted new names, some figures were assimilated to similar figures in Italian story and religion, while others kept their outward form but underwent a change of style or meaning. The change from the Greek 'Heracles' to his Roman form as 'Hercules' involves more a change in emphasis than a change in the details of the myth. The only major Roman addition to the great body of stories about Heracles involved an incident when Heracles was completing one of his Labours, the capture of the cows of Geryon. He is said to have stopped in Italy, at the site on which Rome would one day be built, and saved the cattle from an attempt to steal them. The story is told by the Roman poet Virgil in Book 8 of the *Aeneid*, and formed the *aetion*, the cult explanation, for the altar of Hercules in the centre of Rome at the Forum Boarium, The Cattle Market.[12] The position of Hercules in the great epic created under the auspices of the first Roman Emperor Augustus is an indication of the political capital to be gained from Hercules' image. The link to the Forum Boarium indicates the geographical centrality of Hercules to Roman life, which was mirrored by the way he was assimilated to the core values of Roman identity, *virtus* and Stoicism.[13]

For the Romans Hercules became the exemplar of Stoic virtue. The philosophy of Stoicism was originally Greek, and advocated an attitude towards life which accepted hardships with devotion to struggle and duty.[14] In Rome it became adapted to emphasise a number of national standards such as bravery, forbearance and civic duty. The moral, intellectual strength of Hercules was brought to the fore, and he was used as a model by several powerful figures in the Republic and the Empire. Augustus likened himself to Hercules as a figure of civic strength, while later emperors were more explicit: Nero performed as Hercules, and Commodus was said to have dressed as Hercules, claiming he was the reincarnation of the hero.[15]

Despite his attraction as a political strongman, it was no small matter to downplay all the other aspects of Hercules/Heracles' persona and the incidents of dubious moral character. The Epicurean, and thus anti-Stoic, poet Lucretius attacked this point directly when he compared Hercules unfavourably to his own hero, Epicurus. Lucretius argued that Hercules only killed physical monsters in the external world, which sensible people could have avoided, but Epicurus found a way to tame the internal monsters of the mind, terrors which we cannot simply escape by physical force.[16]

9. After Euripides

Seneca's *Hercules Furens*

This, then, is the context in which Euripides' play found its closest descendant, the *Hercules Furens* (*Mad Hercules*) by Seneca.[17] A Stoic philosopher, political advisor to the emperor Nero, and prolific playwright, Seneca produced many plays reworking themes which had been treated by the Greek playwrights, adding a particularly Roman, Stoic flavour. In addition to his *Hercules Furens* he also wrote a version of Hercules' death, *Hercules Oetaeus*, the story previously told in Sophocles' *Women of Trachis*. When compared to Euripides' version, Seneca's play can be viewed as excessive, loud, and lacking in subtlety. Many of the details which gave Euripides' play its depth have been changed or omitted. One example will indicate the scale of the alteration. In Seneca's play the children are an afterthought for the tyrant Lycus who is focused on Megara. When she refuses to marry him he decides to burn 'you and all your flock' (*Hercules Furens*, vv. 507-8). The tensions surrounding the children's role which we discussed in Chapter 5 are missing entirely. While Euripides' play is the strongest source for Seneca's version there can be little doubt that many other works of literature had an influence, and these may include other dramatised versions of the story which have not survived.

The Roman play has its own interest, not least in the question of whether Seneca intended the play to be a clearly moral, Stoic story, an illustration of the need to control the emotions.[18] Most modern critics view Hercules' motivation as his obsession with conquest and self-image, but Billerbeck argues that the focus is on Juno's decision to use the Furies to attack him.[19] However we interpret the play, it is clearly a very different treatment of the myth from Euripides' version. Why, then, should Seneca's drama be relevant to this discussion?

The Western world

In considering the survival of Euripides' play, we must remember that it was through familiarity with Roman versions that later Western culture received most of its Greek culture.

Not until the Renaissance did Greek tragedies receive attention in their own rights, and even after that point Roman material was far more widely accessible. Shakespeare was directly influenced by Seneca rather than by Greek plays, so we should be aware of the power of Roman ideas when we assess the formation of Western drama.[20] Euripides' *Heracles* did not have any particular reason to survive as a prominent part of the Heracles myth, and the filtering of the play via Seneca's version was likely to eclipse the Greek original. The survival of the play to the present day may be due to a number of features, such as the popularity of Heracles/Hercules as a mythological figure across the centuries, but *Heracles* was not one of the plays singled out for praise and retention in the ancient world.

The current texts we have of tragedy today can be traced back to manuscripts produced in the ninth or tenth century CE, but the process of transmission and selection before that date is difficult to assess. Scholarly consensus is that at some point, probably in the Byzantine period *c*. ninth century CE, twenty-three plays were chosen for concerted copying and preservation, seven by Aeschylus, seven by Sophocles and nine by Euripides. *Heracles* was not one of the plays selected, so its survival owes more to chance. A partial manuscript from the fourteenth century preserved a number of plays by Euripides; some duplicate the selected plays and some, including *Heracles*, would not otherwise have survived. The section of manuscript presented an alphabetical list and *Heracles* is one of the plays in 'E' (*Erakles Mainomenos* in Greek).[21] This method of transmission tells us nothing about the importance attached to the story or its value for different audiences, but the theological speculations which close the drama may also have contributed to the play's survival, as they spoke to a number of ideas and lines of interpretations which developed during later periods.

From Rome to the twentieth century

The history of our particular play, and dramatised versions of Heracles' story, will only come into focus towards the end of this section. We will begin by noting the general trends which ensured the survival of stories of Heracles. The first question to consider is how any mythology from the Graeco-Roman world survived after the fall of the Roman Empire and the establishment of the narratives of Christianity. Without the foundation of the polytheistic Olympian religion, how could the myth survive, when Christianity rapidly became a dominant force which disapproved of the theological and moral stance implied by many mythological stories? Seznec indicates the range of issues which occasioned the transmission of the stories.[22]

Firstly, the survival of widely known literary treatments was instrumental in many cases. Literary texts became central to the educational process as a knowledge of Greek and Latin became the mark of the privileged elite. Furthermore, some stories survived because of the inherent malleability of myth which we discussed in Chapter 2. This is certainly true for Heracles, whose stories were re-interpreted in terms more acceptable to Christian values. The multiple ancient views of Heracles as drunken buffoon/ethical exemplar moved him from the area of philosophy into the area of religion, and Heracles' interaction with Christianity produced a variety of different approaches to the material. The Christian fathers were keen to dismiss any rivals to the position of Christ, and so downplayed Heracles' ethical side, portraying him more as the simple strongman, much as Lucretius had done from his Epicurean standpoint. However, at the opposite extreme, Dante explicitly compared Heracles to Christ in the motif of the descent to Hell.[23] The philosophical strand of Heracles' persona also continued to develop, as the myths of his life were popular subjects for allegorists. Individual episodes and attributes from Heracles' story were frequently reformulated, relating the actions and symbols to particular brands of philosophy. The murder of the children, for example, was discussed by Coluccio Salutati, the famous scholar of the fifteenth century; he produced a narrative account with the children represented as physical vices, and thus cast Heracles' actions in killing them in a more positive, symbolic light.[24]

In wider culture, Heracles, as we noted in the Greek context, could be used as the popular type of 'strong man/action hero'.

In this respect, he had similarities to many other 'strong man' figures in folktale such as Samson, and thus had some universal relevance.[25] The sheer number of stories about Heracles also made his mythology a good source for storytellers, and the idea of madness has inspired literature throughout the centuries.[26] Reid Davidson lists hundreds of items in her catalogue of uses of the Heracles figure in Western Arts between 1300 and 1900, which indicate the range of interest in all aspects of the figure.[27] 'In the theatre, however, Heracles' appearances have been few and far between, most notably in *The Silver Age*, staged in 1613 by Thomas Heywood, a play which dramatised several episodes of the hero's life. While individual instantiations of the myth may not immediately spring to mind when a modern audience hears the name 'Heracles', the long period of transmission and reformulation of the myth created the popular opinions and dominant trends which provide a wider background for readers/viewers approaching the play today. To reprise the critical problem outlined in the introduction to this volume, if we take the 'perceptual filters' approach of Sourvinou-Inwood, we may attempt to step back from our world to the ancient world, as much of this volume has attempted to do.[28] However, many would argue that it is impossible to look at material from anything other than our own viewpoints, and that we should instead be paying greater attention to the process of transmission and the vast range of material which stands between us and the ancient texts.

Into the twenty-first century

Where, then, do Heracles and Euripides' play fit into the modern world? The intervening years have paradoxically given modern audiences a greater range of images than that available to the original audience, and yet created the simplified category of 'superhero'. It is as the symbol of strength and dynamism that his name is given to planes, such as the military transport plane the 'C-130 Hercules', or the several Royal Navy ships which have gone by this title. The ethical side of the story has been largely eclipsed by the action-hero model, as, for example, in Arnold Schwarzenegger's 1970 film *Hercules in New York*, a mixture of animation and fantasy which showed little concern for psychological subtlety.[29] In earlier chapters we explored the concept of heroism, noting differences between modern and ancient views of the term. If, however, we put aside the general usage of the phrase, and look instead at dramatic contexts, we can see that it is not impossible for *Heracles* to find a home in modern Western culture. Just as tragedy was a powerful form of storytelling in fifth-century Athens, so today television and film provide a home for similar accounts. Dramatic superheroes, such as Superman, Batman or Buffy, may be primarily action heroes, but the narratives also rely on creating internal tensions for the characters, often to do with identity and their place in the 'real world' when the villains are no more. One of the newest, modern myths comes from George Lucas' *Star Wars* films, which have a strong moral content around issues of family and friendship.[30] While these stars of the screen may not embody the same extreme dichotomy as seen in the fifth-century Athenian Heracles, there are enough parallels for the physical strength/personal difficulties type of story for Euripides' tale to find a place in the modern psyche.

When the modern superhero was being created around the period of the Second World War (Superman first appeared in 1938), Hercules became a popular figure in wider culture. There were two comic book series about him, including the Blue Ribbon comics, a short series of comics under the title 'Hercules, Modern Champion of Justice'. In taking on Nazis and corrupt government officials Hercules became once again the scourge of society's evils.[31] In the same climate Agatha Christie published a series of short stories between 1939 and 1940, later published as a single volume entitled *The Labours of Hercules: The Legend of Poirot's Retirement*.[32] While the central conceit of solving twelve cases each with some link to a Labour needs little comment, the incidental details of the presentation are more telling, particularly for the reception of Euripides' play. A passage from the foreword gives an interesting glimpse of the state of scholarship:

Take this Hercules – this hero! Hero, indeed! What was he but a large muscular creature of low intelligence and criminal tendencies! Poirot was reminded of one Adolfe Durand, a butcher, who had been tried at Lyon in 1895 – a creature of oxlike strength who had killed several children. The defence had been epilepsy – from which he undoubtedly suffered – though whether *grand mal* or *petit mal* had been an argument of several days' discussion. This ancient Hercules probably suffered from *grand mal*. No, Poirot shook his head, if *that* was the Greeks' idea of a hero, then measured by modern standards it certainly would not do.[33]

Poirot continues to draw a contrast between himself and Hercules, but then comes to see a resemblance: 'Both of them, undoubtedly, had been instrumental in ridding the world of certain pests ... Each of them could be described as a benefactor to the Society he lived in.'[34]

For our study of Euripides' *Heracles*, this reference to the madness is striking. It is the first episode from Heracles' life which the novel refers to explicitly, even though it is not part of the Labours. Furthermore, despite the apparently simple terms in which the opposition/resemblance is established, there is nonetheless a complex negotiation of relationship between ancient and modern: the real life case of Durand is used to explain the ancient model, and yet for all his rejection of ancient models of behaviour Poirot still comes to accept Heracles as his prototype for his crowning glory. This awareness of the paradoxes of the myth is placed within a context of the privileges of classical learning, for Poirot is inspired to begin his research when he talks to an academic and regrets his lack of a classical education:

And Poirot, watching him, felt suddenly a doubt – an uncomfortable twinge. Was there, here, something that he had missed? Some richness of the spirit? Sadness crept over him. Yes, he should have become acquainted with the Classics ... Long ago ... Now, alas, it was too late ...[35]

The motif of the Labours is linked throughout the novel with several more explicit references to the role of the Classics in society. There is also a reworking of ideas of fathers and sons and the diagnosis of madness in chapter 7, *The Cretan Bull*. This use of a mythological character, critical speculation and all, indicates a mood at the time when scholarship was arguing for the epilepsy line (see above, Chapter 6). The ancient world, and the role of Classics in education, was under increasing scrutiny and censure, but modern readers were still happy to appropriate the material for their own ends.[36]

The critical process

The history of scholarship on the play is punctuated by a number of strong figures and responses to wider intellectual trends. A brief summary will indicate the trends explored in more detail in specific chapters. At the start of the twentieth century, critics such as Wilamowitz saw the madness as inherent to Heracles' own character and he has been followed by others such as Kamerbeek, although Wilamowitz later changed his mind on this issue. The play has not received great scholarly attention, but has moved with changing trends in work on tragedy in general. The madness and its psychological causes have been explored by critics such as Griffiths, Simon and Slater, who draw on the psychoanalytic literary criticism developed first by figures such as Lacan.[37] This work has affinities with a greater interest in the domestic structures of tragedy and the patriarchal system which supports it.[38] The broken structure of the play has found new appreciation when viewed through post-structuralist, deconstructionist lenses drawing on the work of Derrida.[39] Dunn has suggested that the play has a novelistic quality about it and is essentially best appreciated via the work of Bakhtin.[40] The most valuable strand of criticism for this play may well be the increased interest in issues of staging, and the understanding of texts as only one part of a theatrical performance. Drawing upon the work of Taplin and others, a number of recent articles have explored the play's physical presence, with Worman's discussion of the corporeal/metaphorical yokes in the play, George's analysis of the symbolism of the gaze, and Rehm's exploration of the architecture of the play and its use of the physical house.[41]

The play as theatre

The *Oxford Archive of Performances of Greek and Roman Drama* currently knows of twenty-three modern productions of *Heracles*, the earliest in 1745 in England, followed by two amateur productions, one in England in 1818 and one in Greece in 1879.[42] The late nineteenth and early twentieth centuries witnessed a revival in the popularity and production of Greek tragedy, connected to the resurgence in scholarship. Gilbert Murray's range of English translations were used for performance in the early twentieth century, and scholarship in German inspired a number of significant productions: a German translation was staged in Austria in 1902, and further productions followed the publication in 1959 of Wilamowitz's monumental edition of the play. [43]

In the twentieth century the play received worldwide attention with productions throughout Europe, the USA and Japan. This range of productions is not great when compared to the popularity of other Euripidean plays such as *Medea*.[44] Nevertheless, the global range of the productions does indicate some degree of relevance for modern audiences. In the UK, the King's College Greek Play staged *Heracles* in 1959, only five years after the first KCL Greek play. The play has been revived in this arena on a number of occasions, including the production of 1983, culminating in a tour of North America with a play about Heracles, which combined material from a number of plays including Euripides' *Heracles*. In this one twentieth-century English theatrical tradition alone the play has received more outings than many other plays, despite its strange, controversial subject matter and style.

To close our examination of the play's production history, we will compare three late twentieth-century versions and consider their response to historical and social conditions in the period; but something must first be said about Disney's animated story, *Hercules*, for it is likely that this cartoon will have a significant effect on the way future audiences come to Euripides' play. If the first time you meet Hercules he is a cartoon figure in a Disney movie, this is the image which is likely to colour your later perceptions, and puts him into the same mental category as Snow White and a clownfish called Nemo. The film has its critics – it was not a huge hit with children, nor with the purists who blanched at the film's mix-and-match approach to the ancient world. However, a number of points are interesting for the student of Euripides' play. Firstly, in the Disney story Hercules faces a moral dilemma and only prevails by combining his physical strength with ethical strength. Secondly, although the film has many comic elements, these are not usually generated from the figure of Hercules himself, but from subsidiary characters. Finally, Disney introduces a new element to the myths with the character of Philoctetes who provides the young Hercules with guidance and training. In the Greek versions the lack of consistent education was a striking feature of the story of Heracles when compared to the early histories of other great figures, and provided some explanation for his untrained, violent behaviour in adult life. With the character of Philoctetes Disney could be seen as rectifying Heracles' character problem – an indication of the modern faith in education perhaps? If these are the contributions made by the twentieth century to the reception of Heracles the character, what then of *Heracles* the play?

Some productions have tried to let the text and the power of the story touch a modern audience directly. Nick Philippou's production of the play at the Gate Theatre, London, in 1998 worked in a small studio space where the audience sat on benches close to the action. The staging was simple, and focused on the use of large staffs by the Chorus to create musical and tonal effects. The play kept to a simple translation by Kenneth McLeish which allowed the action to speak for itself. The audience was forced to contemplate the horror of the situation in itself, without any need to explore their own immediate political or psychological circumstances. The great physicality and immediacy of the play conveyed a general message of fear and horror. The key themes of the production were explicit in the programme notes, which commented:

This abrupt, bleak ending focuses attention on the play's great themes, the two questions which occur time and again in Euripides' work ... 'How can mortals find a way to live in a universe controlled by gods who we find aloof or actively hostile?' and 'How can we cope with death?'

By contrast, two other twentieth-century productions have contained a great deal of guidance and interpretation in their translation and performance of the play. Riley has discussed the 1965 University of Chicago *Heracles*, produced by Archibald MacLeish in connection with Armitage's late twentieth-century play *Mister Heracles*.[45] She argues that the plays respond to immediate issues of social concern, and can thus tell us more about the modern audience than the ancient one. MacLeish's production was a reworking of the play with direct reference in the text and visual staging to the political climate of the Cold War, and the message of the story was about the danger of taking on god-like powers. MacLeish clearly felt a strong connection to the story, as he returned to the play after it was not well received in its first productions. The version which he published contained an additional new first act with modern characters which allowed him to explore more directly the social tensions he saw played out in *Heracles*. Riley suggests that, in MacLeish's reading, the play is indicative of a society on the cusp of major changes in sexual and national politics. These changes, she argues, were fully digested by the time Simon Armitage produced his *Mister Heracles*, a play which is far more explicit in its examination of the gender-dynamics to the story. Armitage's play makes a number of significant verbal and contextual changes to the text, but the play aims to be a direct response to Euripides' *Heracles*, rather than to wider traditions about the figure of Heracles. The basic outline of the plot structure remains, but the language is at times updated and certain key details are changed. For example, the Chorus relates the Labours as modern events, as Heracles solves crises such as nuclear explosions or flesh-eating viruses. Furthermore, when Heracles kills his children there is no mention of any idea that he thinks they are Eurystheus' children. The visual impact was central to the overall message: Heracles arrived on stage in a space suit, emphasising the alien nature of the world in which he worked. The analogy is interesting, for modern viewers accept the existence of the space programme and the actions of heroic astro/cosmonauts without having any direct experience. It is an act of faith not entirely dissimilar from that of ancient Greek audiences who believed in mythological figures. The Chorus of the play articulate an idea only implicit in the original when they respond to Heracles' return home:

> *Hard to be a hero out in the world*
> and the same hero back in your own home[46]

The production, as directed by Natasha Betteridge for the West Yorkshire Playhouse in 2001, made it clear that its theme was the impact of militarism. The immediate contemporary reference made by a number of critics was the violence brought home by war veterans. In this way the play was related to a particular set of concerns about the violence of the modern world.

Riley's examination of this production has also highlighted the examination of heroism and militarism in terms of gendered analysis:

> ... The women's movement of the 1970s, and the growing conviction that women's status and role cannot be understood without analysing the role of men, have aided the rediscovery of Euripides' Heracles in the late twentieth and early twenty-first centuries and profoundly affected our reading of the filicide.[47]

Gender-sensitive readings of the play cast new light on the role of Megara, the good wife who nonetheless dies, breaking the traditional tragic pattern, as we explored in Chapter 5. It also creates a new discursive space for us to explore the place of the myth of Heracles within Greek culture. Loraux's analysis of the ambiguous sexuality of Heracles, from extreme masculinity to extreme femininity,[48] now takes on more than mythological significance as we examine the centrality of normative gender structures in an ordered society. Riley draws attention to the reevaluation of Heracles and Medea as male and female paradigms of the child killer, noting how Tony Harrison's production *Medea: A Sex War Opera* closes by questioning society's fixation with Medea, and turning the spotlight on to Heracles: Medea is vilified for her actions, but Heracles maintains a largely positive reputation in the ancient and modern world. As we discussed in Chapter 2, there are strong similarities between the figures of Heracles and Ino, an association which is given greater meaning when we approach it with the tools of feminist analysis, an approach taken by Doherty and others in recent work on ancient mythology.[49] The play which has survived through centuries as a written artefact is now being revived through re-performance, and the physical existence of the play as drama is inviting a new audience to engage with it as part of their own lives – quite an achievement for a play written for a single performance in the fifth century BCE.

Conclusion

For the fifth-century Athenian audience the story of Heracles' madness raised issues about their own social structures in a time of war, and of the place of man in the divine scheme. It is interesting to note that recent interpretations of the play have conflated the two ideas: the ancient Heracles had no protection from an unseen force striking from afar, whereas the modern Heracles has no protection from having a bomb dropped on him. It may be that the human forces of the military and the government are just as mysterious and dangerous to us today as were the Olympian gods to the fifth-century Greeks. For modern audiences, then, the story of Euripides' *Heracles* can transcend the centuries and pose new questions together with the old, ultimately returning to question who are the heroes and who are our gods.

Notes

1. Introduction

1. Disney's animated film *Hercules* (1997, directed by R. Clements & J. Musker) will be discussed more fully in the final chapter. The volume of poetry *Hercules and the Birds* by Bikshu Sthavira Sangharakshita, the founder of the Western Buddhist Order, contains a long poem about the challenges of life inspired by the statue of Hercules Farnese, which makes particular play with the murder of the children.

2. See Garland, *Surviving Greek Tragedy*.

3. The seminal essay by Jung is available as a separate text translated by R.F.C. Hull as *The Archetypes and the Collective Unconscious*. Lang produced three important treatises explaining his method: *Custom and Mythology*, 2nd ed. (London: Longman's, 1885), *Myth, Ritual and Religion*, 2nd ed. (London: Longman's, 1899), and *The Making of Religion* (London: Longman's, 1899).

4. On the challenge to universal views, see Cahan, Mechling, Sutton Smith & White, 'The Elusive Historical Child'.

5. A good place to start analysing the differences between ancient and modern ideas is Aldrete, *Gestures and Acclamations in Ancient Rome*.

6. King, *Hippocrates' Woman*.

7. The key article on the issue of Heracles' sexuality is Loraux, 'Herakles: The Super-Male and the Feminine'.

8. Sophocles' play does contain a reference to the Freudian structure, when Jocasta tells Oedipus not to worry 'because many men have married their mother in their dreams' (*Oedipus The King* vv. 981-2). Freudian critics would take this as evidence that there is a common psychological trait in the story. It is impossible to escape once we begin to engage with Freudian theory, because any attempt to deny a connection can be dismissed as 'denial' and thus ignored. Critics of Freud's work emphasise the immediate context in which he was writing and even later psychoanalysts who have drawn on his work have generally developed more nuanced readings.

9. Sourvinou-Inwood, *'Reading' Greek Culture*; *'Reading' Greek Death*.

10. Martindale, *Redeeming the Text*; 'Proper Voices: Writing the Writer'.

2. Heracles and Greek Myth

1. On the sources for the myth, see Gantz, *Early Greek Myth*, pp. 374-463.

2. A powerful version of this story of Hera's attack on the infant Heracles can be found in Theocritus' *Idyll* 24, and the significance of this incident as the beginning of Heracles' heroic career is well discussed by Cusset, 'L'enfance'. Cf. Wathelet, 'Les enfances'.

3. On the role of Heracles as the founder of the Dorian race, see Hooker, *The Ancient Spartans*.

4. Plutarch, *On the Malice of Herodotus*. On the ethnic and political associations of Heracles' origins, see Bernal, *Black Athena*. Bernal notes that classical scholarship has often played down the Egyptian, non-Western images of Heracles, even though they appear in numerous artistic representations of the hero.

5. Jourdain-Annequin, *Héraclès aux portes du soir*. Kirk, 'Methodological Reflexions', argues that emphasis on Heracles' conquest of death has been misplaced, and that the hero represents youth rather than immortality. See discussion of related myths in Mathieu, 'Résurrection'.

6. Dumézil, *The Destiny of a King*. On similar lines see Burkert, 'Le Mythe de Géryon'.

7. For links between classical mythology and folktale paradigms, see Hansen, *Ariadne's Thread*.

8. Loraux, *The Experience of Tiresias*.

9. Pralon, *Les travaux d'Héraclès dans L'Héraclès Furieux d'Euripide*.

10. On the Homeric epics, see Ford, *Homer: The Poetry of the Past*; Fowler, *The Cambridge Companion to Homer*; Nagy, *Homeric Responses*; Patzek, *Homer und seine Zeit*.

11. Translated by S. Lombardo, *Homer: Iliad* (Indianapolis: Hackett, 1997).

12. Translated by S. Lombardo, *Homer: Iliad* (Indianapolis: Hackett, 1997).

13. On Heracles' apotheosis, see Holt, 'Herakles' Apotheosis' and Boardman, 'Herakles in extremis'.

14. Kirk, 'Methodological Reflexions'.

15. Bond, *Euripides: Heracles*, p. 154.

16. See Morgan, 'The Sculptures of the Hephaisteion'.

17. On the Madness and the Labours in general, see Pike, 'Hercules Furens'.

18. Pausanias 9.11.2.

19. See Furley, 'Studies'.

20. Apollodorus, *Bibliotheca* 2.4.12. Cf. Nicolaus of Damascus (*F. Gr. Hist* 90 F 13).

21. Wilamowitz, *Euripides*: *Herakles*.

22. The conflict between the Centaurs and Lapiths is set out in the Hesiodic *Aspis* 178-90.

23. On issues of self-control and education, see Jaegar, *Paideia*, and Mathé, 'Les enfants de Cheiron', on the process of education undergone by other heroes.

24. The killing of the music teacher Linus, son of Apollo, is illustrated on a number of fifth-century BCE vases, and may have been the subject of a satyr play *Linos* by the poet Achaeus. The accounts in Diodorus Siculus (3.67.2) and Apollodorus' *Bibliotheca* (2.4.9) tell us that Linus struck Heracles for his failings as a pupil and Heracles killed him in angry retaliation.

25. Apollonius Rhodius *Argonautica* 1.1260ff. (translated by Hunter 1993). See Gantz, *Early Greek Myth*, p. 348 on the possibilities of pre-Hellenistic versions of the Hylas myth.

26. On Pindar's representations of the hero, see Pike, 'Pindar's Treatment of the Heracles Myths'.

27. Kuntz, 'The Prodikean choice of Herakles'. Cf. Rochette, 'Héraclès à la croissé des chemins'.

28. Verbanck-Piérard, 'Le double culte'. See also Lévêque & Verbanck-Piérard, 'Héraclès héros ou dieu?'

29. Jourdain-Annequin, 'A propos d'un rituel'.

30. Lloyd Jones, 'Herakles at Eleusis'. See also Robertson, 'Heracles' catabasis'. There is also a vase which shows Medea and Heracles as related child-murderers at Eleusis, illustrated and discussed by Schmidt, 'Medea und Herakles. Zwei tragische Kindermörder'.

31. Mathieu, 'Résurrection'. See also Pellizer, 'Figures narrative de la mort et l'immortalité'; Wathelet, 'Rhésos'.

32. On the interaction of Heracles, Peisistratus and Eleusis see Boardman, 'Herakles, Peisistratos and Eleusis', and 'Herakles, Peisistratos, and the Unconvinced'. On the Athenian/Spartan interplay in tragic treatments of Heracles, see Vickers, 'Heracles Lacedaemonius'.

33. Winkler, 'The Ephebes' Song'.

34. Armitage, *Mister Heracles*, vii.

35. The link to modern war veterans was made with reference to Armitage's production of the play, by Paul Taylor writing in the *Independent* newspaper, 28 February 2002, p. 10. On similar lines, T. Allen Mills writing in *The Sunday Times*, 28 July 2002, p. 18, begins 'An eruption of domestic violence at one of America's biggest military bases has forced commanders to examine possible connections to the stress of wartime service. Three soldiers who fought with US special forces in Afghanistan have allegedly murdered their wives in the past six weeks at Fort Bragg, North Carolina.'

36. The image of the returning hero disrupting society is explored in the work of Dumézil, *The Destiny of a King*, and Girard, *Mensonge romantique et vérité romanesque* and *The Theater of Envy*. Cf. Gordon, 'Reason and Ritual in Greek Tragedy'.

37. Bowman, unpublished paper to the American Philological Association (2003), abstract available at http://www.apaclassics.org/AnnualMeeting/03mtg/abstracts/bowman.html.

38. On the role of superheroes and the Heracles myth, see T. Geier, 'The incredible hunk vs. cheesy monsters: low-budget Hercules', *U.S. News & World Report* 122.24 (23 June 1997), p. 63.

39. See Fisher, *Hybris*.

40. Since the expulsion of the last tyrant Hippias at the end of the sixth century, Athenian government had come under the control of increasingly large sections of the population, with reformers such as Cleisthenes and Ephialtes introducing reforms which gave political power to the ordinary citizens more than the wealthy elite. For an account of these developments, see Stockton, *The Classical Athenian Democracy*.

41. Pericles' Funeral Speech, as given by Thucydides in his *History of the Peloponnesian War* 2.60-2.

42. The issue of the individual versus the community, and the integration of fighters into society, is as old as the Homeric epics, and continues to be relevant today. See Shay, *Achilles in Vietnam*.

43. On ostracism, see Kagan, 'The Origins and Purpose of Ostracism'.

44. Easterling, 'Constructing the Heroic'.

3. Euripides, Heracles and Greek Tragedy

1. For the detail of staging plays, see Storey & Allen, *A Guide to Ancient Greek Drama*, and the sourcebook Csapo & Slater, *Contexts of Ancient Drama*. On the political aspects of tragedy in Athens, see Goldhill & Osborne, *Performance Culture*.

2. On the processes of transmission, see Easterling, 'From Repertoire to Canon'; Garland, *Surviving Greek Tragedy*.

3. On Cyclops, see Konstan, 'The Anthropology of Euripides' *Kyklops*'.

4. On the disputed authorship of the *Prometheus Bound*, see Conacher, *Aeschylus' Prometheus Bound*; M. Griffith, *Authenticity*.

5. The style of messenger speeches is well discussed by de Jong, *Narrative in Drama*. For the interplay between Homer and Drama, see Easterling, 'The Tragic Homer'; Garner, *From Homer to Tragedy*.

6. On Aeschylus, see Conacher, *Aeschylus*; Sommerstein, *Aeschylean Tragedy*; Taplin, *Stagecraft*.

7. On Sophocles, see Blundell, *Helping Friends*; Buxton, *Sophocles*.

8. On *Philoctetes*, see Park Poe, *Heroism and Divine Justice*; Ussher, *Sophocles: Philoctetes*.

9. On *Alcestis*, see Dyson, 'Alcestis' Children and the Character of Admetus'; Goldfarb, 'The Conflict of Obligations in Euripides' Alcestis'; Lada-Richards, 'Staging the Ephebeia'.

10. Segal, *Euripides and the Poetics of Sorrow*, pp. 69-70.

11. For an overview of the problems, see Marshall, '*Alcestis* and the Problem of Prosatyric Drama'.

12. Stevens, *Colloquial Expressions*.

13. See Berg, 'Alcestis and Hercules'.

14. On the *Women of Trachis*, see Bowman, 'Prophecy and Authority in the *Trachiniae*'; Sorum, 'Monsters and the Family: the Exodus of Sophocles *Trachiniae*'.

15. See Dumanoir, 'La moisson d'Héraklès: le héros, le domaine et les enfants dans Les Trachiniennes'.

16. See Just, *Women in Athenian Law and Life*; Hawley & Levick, *Women in Antiquity*.

17. Translated by Jameson, *Sophocles: Women of Trachis*.

18. Dunn, 'Ends and Means', p. 96 n. 26.

19. Huys, 'Euripides' *Auge*'.

20. Dobrov, *Figures of Play*, chapter 8.

21. See Padel, *Whom the Gods Destroy*.

22. Galinsky, *The Herakles Theme*, p. 81.

23. See Sutton, *The Greek Satyr Play*.

24. Galinsky, *The Herakles Theme*.

25. On Aristophanes' *Frogs*, see Bowie, *Aristophanes: Myth, Ritual and Comedy*; Silk, *Aristophanes and the Definition of Comedy*.

26. On the interplay of Heracles and Dionysus in *Frogs*, see Padilla, 'The Heraclean Dionysus'.

27. See Garland, *Surviving Greek Tragedy*.

28. Segal, *Euripides and the Poetics of Sorrow*.

29. On Euripides' theological standpoint, see Lefkowitz, 'Impiety in Euripides'.

30. See Thucydides, *History of the Peloponnesian War*.

31. On changes in democracy, see Hornblower, *The Greek World*.

32. Disastrous for the poet, that is. The Persian capture of Miletus in 494 was taken as the subject of a play by Phrynichus produced *c.* 490 BCE. Herodotus commented thus:

'The Athenians, on the other hand, showed themselves beyond measure afflicted at the fall of Miletus, in many ways expressing their sympathy, and especially by their treatment of Phrynichus. For when this poet brought out upon the stage his drama *The Capture of Miletus*, the whole theatre burst into tears; and the people sentenced him to pay a fine of a thousand drachmas, for recalling to them their own misfortunes.' Herodotus, *Histories* 6.21 (translated by Rawlinson).

33. Dobrov, *Figures of Play* p. 9.

34. Abel, *Metatheatre*.

35. Plato, *Republic* VII, 514a-521b.

36. Internal evidence includes features of style and, particularly, metre in which an observable historical development is acknowledged (see Cropp & Fick, *Resolutions and Chronology in Euripides: The Fragmentary Tragedies*). Only a handful of plays can be securely dated by external dates such as victor's list (99% conclusive) or references/absence of references to historical events (far less reliable). Other methods of dating, such as attempted correlations between historical events and perceived attitudes displayed within certain plays, can provide insights into trends, but are of very little value in determining precise chronologies.

4. Dramatic Structure and Unity

1. See Bond, *Euripides: Heracles*, p. 146 n. ad 348.

2. Taplin's most influential work is *The Stagecraft of Aeschylus*. Further studies focused on staging issues include Halleran, *Stagecraft in Euripides*; Seale, *Vision and Stagecraft in Sophocles*.

3. See Goldhill, *Reading Greek Tragedy*.

4. Taplin, 'Opening Performance: Closing Texts', p. 93.

5. See the challenging, but rewarding, study of theatrical space in Rehm, *The Play of Space*.

6. On the status of ancient stage directions, see Taplin, 'Did Greek Dramatists Write Stage Instructions?'.

7. See Taplin, 'The Pictorial Record'.

8. The evidence for Greek music is discussed by West, *Ancient Greek Music*.

9. On the use of tableaux in tragedy, see Golder, 'Making a Scene'.

10. A thoughtful discussion of the issue of masking in Greek drama is provided by Walton, *Greek Theatre Practice*, chapter 7.

11. The Athenian cultural ideal was that women should remain indoors and so preserve a pale complexion. As all the actors were male, the differentiation in masking was an additional element in establishing a character's gender.

12. On the iconography of Heracles, see Volkommer, *Herakles in the Art of Classical Greece*.

13. Krauss, 'Dangerous Supplements'.

14. Burnett, *Catastrophe Survived*, pp. 157-82.

15. Although Bond, *Euripides: Heracles*, saw the ode as detached from the action, Rehm has argued persuasively that the ode 'dovetails' well with it. See Rehm, *The Play of Space*, pp. 100ff.

16. Garland, *The Greek Way of Death*, notes that the standard Greek burial outfit was white. Cf. Danforth, *The Death Rituals of Rural Greece*.

17. For the fragments and hypothesis of *Melanippe the Wise*, see Collard, Cropp & Lee, *Euripides. Selected Fragmentary Plays I*, pp. 240-80.

18. The significance of old age in tragedy is discussed by Falkner, 'Euripides and the Stagecraft of Old Age'.

19. See Grummond, 'Heracles' Entrance'.

20. Kovacs, *Euripides*: *Suppliant Women, Electra, Heracles*, p. 355.

21. See Bain, *Masters, Servants and Orders in Greek Tragedy*.

22. The range of comments on movement in tragedy is discussed by Shisler, 'The Use of Stage Business'.

23. Metrical analysis of the choral passages is provided in Bond, *Euripides: Heracles*. Although the basic metre of tragic is the iambic trimeter, choral odes employ a variety of different lyric metres to achieve different effects. See West, *Greek Metre*.

24. This dramatic structure, of a joyful choral ode just before the revelation of disaster, is seen particularly in Sophocles' plays: *Ajax* 693ff., *Women of Trachis* 633ff., *Antigone* 1115ff., *Oedipus the King* 1086ff.

25. See Marshall, 'Some Fifth Century Masking Conventions'.

26. See Arnott, 'Off-stage Cries'; Hamilton, 'Cries Within'.

27. Higgins, 'Deciphering Time'.

28. Niobe boasted that she had more children than Leda, and in revenge the children of Leda, Apollo and Artemis killed all of Niobe's children. Niobe wasted away in ceaseles grief until she was turned to stone. Achilles hid his head in his tent when Agamemnon dishonoured him (events at the start of Homer's *Iliad*), and Aeschylus famously portrayed Achilles muffled on stage.

29. Medea is also compared to a rock in Euripides' *Medea*. On the inadequacy of imagery in that play, see Boedeker, 'Becoming Medea'; Sourvinou-Inwood, 'Images and Euripidean Tragedy'.

30. Porter, *Only Connect*.

31. Rehm, *The Play of Space*, p. 108.

32. Rehm, *The Play of Space*, p. 106.

33. Worman, 'The Ties That Bind'. Cf. the significance of clothing in the *Oresteia* of Aeschylus, discussed by Macleod, 'Clothing in the *Oresteia*'; Tarkow, 'Thematic Implications of Costuming in the *Oresteia*'.

34. Rehm, *The Play of Space*, p. 104.

35. On Euripidean imagery, see Barlow, *The Imagery of Euripides*.

36. On animal imagery generally in Homer, see Schnapp-Gourbeillon, *Lions, héros, masques*.

37. In the *Iliad* Hector is also described as having 'gorgon-eyes', *Iliad* 8.349.

38. Padilla, *The Gorgonic Archer*.

39. Kosak, *Heroic Measures*.

40. Devereux, 'The Self-blinding of Oedipus'; Steiner, 'Stoning and Sight'.

41. Assaël, 'L'Héraclès d'Euripide'.

42. Murray, *Greek Studies*, p. 112.

43. Aristotle *Poetics* 1449b: 'Tragedy endeavours, as far as possible, to confine itself to a single revolution of the sun, or but slightly to exceed this limit.' On the *Poetics*, see a range of approaches in Rorty, *Essays on Aristotle's Poetics*.

44. Older approaches to unity can be seen in Kamerbeek, 'Unity and Meaning'. See also Shelton, 'Structural Unity', who argues that a form of unity comes from ideas of mortality, but also that the disjunctions are deliberate: 'Euripides created abrupt transitions and a sequence of sudden dramatic reversals in order to demonstrate that the events of life are unpredictable', p. 101.

45. Papadopoulou, *Studies*, p. 88.

46. Krauss, 'Dangerous Supplements'.

47. Rehm, 'Performing the Chorus'.

5. Family Values

1. See Dumanoir, 'La moisson d'Héraklès'; Sorum, 'Monsters and the Family'.

2. See Belfiore, *Murder Among Friends*.

3. For a general survey of these issues, see Pomeroy, *Families in Classical and Hellenistic Greece*.

4. See Todd, *The Shape of Athenian Law*.

5. Barone, 'L'apaidia'.

6. The relationship between this care of orphans and drama is discussed by Goldhill, 'The Great Dionysia'.

7. Thucydides, *History of the Peloponnesian War* 2.60.

8. For one view of this issue, see Maitland, 'Dynasty and Family in the Athenian City-State'.

9. The only rituals which are shown in tragedy are the observation of funeral and supplicatory rights. Family rites are not usually featured. For a broad view of the relationship between ritual and literature, see Seaford, *Ritual and Reciprocity*.

10. On the importance of genealogy, see Fowler, 'Genealogical Thinking', and the collection of articles edited by Auger & Said, *Généalogies Mythiques*.

11. See Gregory, 'Euripides' *Heracles*' on the issue of dual parentage in the play. There is also a joke about Heracles' double parentage in Aristophanes' *Birds* 1649ff. Adoption was often for pragmatic reasons to ensure the transmission of property. See Rubinstein, *Adoption in*

IVth Century Athens. For wider issues of heredity see Grmek, 'Ideas on Heredity in Greek and Roman Antiquity'.

12. Ebbott, *Imagining Illegitimacy*.

13. On the reception of the myth of Amphitryon as a meditation on concepts of fatherhood, see Maclean, 'The Heirs of Amphitryon'.

14. Griffith, 'The King and Eye'. Cf. the views of drama in Simon, *Tragic Drama and the Family*; Alford, *The Psychoanalytical Theory of Greek Tragedy*.

15. On the role of the nurse in Greek culture, see Pournara-Karydas, *The 'Trophos' from Homer to Euripides*.

16. For example, Aeschylus' *Agamemnon* vv. 72-82 consists of a song by the old men, explaining why they were too old to fight in Troy, stating that the strength of old men is 'nothing more than that of a child'. See Byl, 'Lamentations'.

17. Griffith, 'The King and Eye'.

18. For the mutual obligations of *tropheia*, see Raepsaet, 'Les motivations de la natalité'.

19. See Higgins, *Deciphering Time*, on the way Heracles fails to fulfil his roles in the family, yet cannot end the wider cycle of disasters: the play needs someone 'to integrate temporal experience in such a way to ward off the depression attendant upon endlessly recurrent cycles', p. 92.

20. On issues of the father–son relationship in the play, see further Mikalson, 'Zeus the Father and Heracles the Son in Tragedy'; Padilla, 'Heroic Paternity'.

21. On reported speech in tragedy, see Bers, *Speech in Speech*.

22. This image is frequently taken to indicate solely the dependence of the children on their father. However, the type of small boat in question, in the Greek *epholkis*, was part of the ship's company and so was useful to the main ship as well as being protected by it. Thus, the image stresses the interdependency of father and children. See further Griffiths, 'Euripides' *Herakles* and the Pursuit of Immortality'.

23. The closest parallels come from Euripides' *Medea* when Medea talks to her sons, vv. 1076ff., and Euripides' *Iphigeneia in Aulis* when Iphigeneia recalls how her father used to play with her as a child, vv. 1219ff. On children in tragedy, see Menu, 'L'enfant'.

24. Rivier, *Essai*, p. 104: 'plus fort que la douleur paternelle, c'est le sentiment d'une faute irrémissible et la honte du déshonneur'.

25. The duties of a wife are outlined in detail in a fifth-century source, Xenophon's *Oeconomicus*.

26. For Greek ideas about the stepmother role, see Watson, *Ancient Stepmothers*. See also Slater, *The Glory of Hera*.

27. For the political, historical context of Thucydides' account of this episode, see Orwin, *The Humanity of Thucydides*.

28. See Dyson & Lee, 'The Funeral of Astyanax'.

29. See Huys, *The Tale of the Hero who was Exposed at Birth*. The debate about the status and frequency of the historical practice of exposure is still ongoing. For a number of different perspectives see Huys, 'The Terminology of Infant Exposure'.

30. Foley, *Ritual Irony*, pp. 167-75.

31. Michelini, *Euripides and the Tragic Tradition*.

32. Dunn, 'Ends and Means'.

33. George, 'Euripides' *Heracles* 140-235', p. 146.

34. Ebbott, *Imagining Illegitimacy*, p. 49.

6. Violence and Madness

1. See Arnott, 'Off-stage Cries'; Hamilton, 'Cries Within'.

2. On *Philoctetes*, see Ussher, *Sophocles: Philoctetes*.

3. Bond, *Euripides: Heracles*, p. 179 n. ad 813.

4. On Lyssa, see Duchemin, 'Le personage de Lyssa'. On Greek personifications, see Stafford, *Worshipping Virtues*.

5. Lee, 'The Iris–Lyssa Scene'.

6. Slater, *The Glory of Hera*.

7. Compare the similar phrasing at Euripides' *Iphigeneia in Tauris*, v. 12 'crown of beautiful glory'.

8. See Hera's attack on Semele, referred to in Euripides' *Bacchae*, or the attack on Io, who is transformed into a cow and tormented by a gadfly (as seen in Aeschylus' *Prometheus Bound*).

9. On the Lycurgus myth and Aeschylus' *Lycourgeia*, which some have suggested was an influence over Euripides' *Heracles*, see Gantz, *Early Greek Myth*, pp. 113-14.

10. On Ajax, see the volume in this series by Hesk, *Ajax*.

11. See Hartigan, 'Euripidean Madness'.

12. Padel, *In and Out of the Mind, Whom the Gods Destroy*. On medicine in tragedy, see Collinge, 'Medical Terms'; Kosak, *Heroic Measures*.

13. Many have argued that there are strong similarities between Ajax and Heracles. See Barlow, 'Sophocles' *Ajax*'.

14. The phrasing of how the madness overcomes Heracles implies something about the way it is conceptualised. For example, Franzino, 'Euripides' *Heracles* 858-73', suggests that Lyssa/madness 'enters' Heracles.

15. Bond, *Euripides' Heracles*, p. 309 n. ad 930-1009.

16. See Collinge, 'Medical Terms', Kosak; *Heroic Measures*.

17. See Shamun, 'Significaciones de Taragma'.

18. See Padilla, 'The Gorgonic Archer'.

19. Filhol, 'Hérakleié nosos'.

20. Hartigan, 'Euripidean Madness', p. 127.

21. Hartigan, 'Euripidean Madness', p. 128.

22. Bond, *Euripides' Heracles* p. 285 n. ad 841f.

23. Bataille, 'Le fou et le devin', p. 150.

24. Burnett, *Catastrophe Survived*.

25. Wilamowitz, *Euripides: Herakles* vol. 2, 127ff.

26. Kirk, 'Methodological Reflexions'.

27. Fitzgerald, 'The Euripidean Heracles'.

28. Krauss, 'Dangerous Supplements'.

29. See Watson, 'Ancient Stepmothers'.

30. See Parker, 'Gods Cruel and Kind' on tragic and divine envy, noting that Hera's envy is of a new kind in Euripides' play.

31. Silk, 'Heracles and Greek Tragedy'.

32. See Shelton, 'Structural Unity'; Griffiths, 'Euripides' *Herakles*'.

33. Lee, 'Iris–Lyssa scene'.

7. Suicide and the Gods

1. On reciprocity, see Seaford, *Reciprocity and Ritual*.

2. The perversion of sacrificial rites is a common motif in Greek tragedy. See Foley, *Ritual Irony*; Zeitlin, 'The Motif of the Corrupted Sacrifice'.

3. Garrison, *Groaning Tears*.

4. On the chosen death of Menoiceus (Euripides' *Phoenician Women*) and Macaria (Euripides' *Children of Heracles*), see Wilkins, 'The State and the Individual: Euripides' Plays of Voluntary Self-Sacrifice'.

5. Yunis, 'A New Creed: Herakles'.

6. De Romilly, 'Le refus du suicide'.

7. Garrison, *Groaning Tears*, p. 75.

8. Fitzgerald, 'The Euripidean Heracles'.

9. See Babut, 'Xenophane's critique'; Lesher, *Xenophanes of Colophon*.

10. Papadopoulou, *Studies*; Lawrence, 'The God that is Truly God'.

11. Electra dismisses the idea that she could judge the return of her brother Orestes by comparing a lock of hair and a footprint (the way the recognition was achieved in Aeschylus' earlier version of the story in *The Libation Bearers*). However, the signs do indeed indicate the return of Orestes, as Electra later discovers.

12. The phrase 'Zeus, whoever he may' be occurs in Aeschylus' *Agamemnon* v. 160.

13. On the links in Greek visual imagery, see Moore, 'Athena and Herakles'.

14. Athena in Aeschylus' *Eumenides* champions the rights of men because she was born from a father without a mother.

15. On Athena in Ajax, see Papadopoulou, 'Athena in Greek Tragedy'.

16. See Neils, 'Athene. Alter Ego of Zeus'.

17. Papadopoulou, 'Athena in Greek Tragedy', notes that Athena appears here both as an epic figure and as Athena Polias (Athena of the City).

8. Theseus and the Role of Friendship

1. 55-9, translated by Davie.

2. Aristotle, *Nichomachean Ethics* 8 & 9, *Eudemian Ethics* 7. See also the discussion of friendship in Plato's *Lysis*, and discussion in Annas, 'Friendship'.

3. Millett, *Lending and Borrowing*, p. 118.

4. Konstan, *Friendship in the Classical World*, p. 57.

5. Euripides' *Orestes* 1155.

6. Konstan, *Friendship in the Classical World*, p. 59.

7. Theseus' double parentage is explained in Apollodorus, *Bibliotheca* 3.15.7. See Boulogne, 'Les double paternités'.

8. Dobrov, *Figures of Play*, chapter 7.

9. See Woodford, *The Cults of Herakles in Attica*.

10. On the Hephaesteum, see Morgan, 'The Sculptures of the Hephaisteion'.

11. Hall, 'The Sociology of Athenian Tragedy', pp. 100-3.

12. See Calame, *Thésée*; Mills, *Theseus, Tragedy and the Athenian Empire*.

13. Loraux, *The Invention of Athens*. The positive portrayal of Athens in this respect can be seen in a number of sources, such as the late fifth- / early fourth-century writer Xenophon in his *Memories of Socrates* 3.5.10, who calls Athens 'a sanctuary for victims of oppression'. Cf. the Funeral Orations of the fourth-century orator Demosthenes, 18.186; 60.8.

14. Konstan, *Friendship in the Classical World*, pp. 83-7.

15. Burnett, *Catastrophe Survived*; Foley, *Ritual Irony*.

16. Michelini, *Euripides and the Tragic Tradition*.

17. Heracles' response to Theseus' offer is to say 'A thousand thanks. But then again, I accomplished a thousand labours' (1353ff.). Bond, *Euripides: Heracles*, p. 404 n. ad 1353, notes the phrasing of the Greek implies a momentary pause and an assertion that the gifts offered are his of right, rather than charity.

18. For the myths of Theseus see Gantz, *Early Greek Myth*, pp. 249-98; Sourvinou-Inwood, *Theseus as Son and Stepson*.

19. See Gantz, *Early Greek Myth*, pp. 264-70.

20. See Gantz, *Early Greek Myth*, pp. 276-7.

21. Mills, *Theseus, Tragedy and the Athenian Empire*.

22. Walker, *Theseus and Athens*.

23. On Orestes, see Hartigan, 'Euripidean Madness'.

24. Dunn, 'Ends and Means', p. 90.
25. Dunn, 'Ends and Means', p. 102.
26. Sfyroeras, 'The Ironies of Salvation'.
27. See discussion of the vase in Schmidt, 'Medea und Herakles'.
28. See Parker, *Miasma*.
29. On the dating of the play from consideration of stylistic and metrical features, see Cropp & Fick, *Resolutions*.
30. Lee, 'The Iris–Lyssa Scene'.
31. Papadopoulou, *Studies*.
32. Rehm, 'Performing the Chorus'.
33. On this topic, see Handley, 'Aristophanes and the Athenian Generation Gap'; Forrest, 'An Athenian Generation Gap'.
34. Thucydides, *History of the Peloponnesian War*, Books 6 & 7.
35. Changing ideas of immortality are discussed by Jaeger, 'The Greek Idea of Immortality'.

9. After Euripides

1. Galinsky, *The Herakles Theme*.
2. Allan, 'Euripides in Megalê Hellas'.
3. The South Italian practice of burying elaborately decorated vases with their dead has preserved many vases showing theatrical scenes. It appears that for personal reasons some people had a particular interest in drama, which their relatives chose to honour in their choice of funeral ware.
4. See Carpenter, *Art and Myth in Ancient Greece*, p. 121, illustrated in fig. 172 p. 135. Boardman notes three other images which show Heracles threatening violence to what may be a child of his own. (*Lexicon Iconographicum Mythologiae Classicae* vol. 4, 'Herakles', pp. 83-6). The catalogue also notes two literary references to visual depictions: an image of Heracles in remorse after the murders in a painting by Nearchus, referred to by Pliny, *Natural History* 35, 141, and an image (possibly imaginary) referred to in Philostratus, *Imagines* 2, 23, showing Heracles seeking out Megara and a third child after killing the first two.
5. That the scene may have a theatrical flavour is suggested by the detailed sections of buildings in the scene. Architectural elements of composition in vase painting are often taken as an indication that what is being shown is a staged scene, rather than simply an imagined episode from mythology.
6. On the mythological symbolism of fire in connection with issues of mortality, see Furley, *Studies in the Use of Fire*; Vernant, 'At Man's Table'.
7. For an indication of the broader spread, assimilation and parallels with the Heracles myth, see Bonnét, *MELQART: Cultes et mythes de l'Héraclès Tyrien en méditerranée*.

8. Theocritus *Idyll* 17.1-33 depicts Alexander deified in the company of Heracles.

9. For a lively discussion of Alexander, see Lane Fox, *Alexander the Great*.

10. See Smith, *Hellenistic Sculpture*, pp. 64-5.

11. See Simon, *Mind and Madness in Ancient Greece*.

12. The story is also used by other Roman poets. See Fedeli, 'Ideologia augustea e poesia: il mito di Ercole e Caco in Properzio'; Janan, 'Refashioning Hercules'. On the role of Hercules in Roman visual art, see S. Ritter, *Hercules in der römischen Kunst von den Anfängen bis Augustus*.

13. The origins of Stoic philosophy lie with Zeno of Citium (336-264 BCE.) For a general discussion of Roman Stoicism, see Boys-Stones, *Post-Hellenistic Philosophy*, a book written in rather a dense style intended for philosophers, but still containing useful information for the non-specialist.

14. Nero appears to have identified strongly with the hero. Suetonius tells us that the part of the mad Hercules was one of the dramatic roles Nero liked to re-enact (*Nero* 20), and that he conceived a plan to perform a Herculean task by killing a lion at the Olympic Games (*Nero* 53).

15. Commodus' Hercules fixation is mentioned by Herodian, 1.14.8, and by Dio Cassius, 73.17. For general discussion of this peculiar figure, see Hesker, *Commodus: An Emperor at the Ccrossroads*. On other Roman uses of the Hercules figure, see Binder, 'Hercules und Claudius'; Rawson, 'Pompey and Hercules'.

16. Lucretius, *De Rerum Natura* (On the Nature of the Universe), 5.1-54.

17. On Seneca's play, see Paratore, *Il prologo dello Hercules furens di Seneca e l'Eracle di Euripide*. On Senecan tragedy more generally, see Boyle, *Tragic Seneca*.

18. Fitch provides a balanced overview of the philosophical aspects of the play, concluding that the while the play was not without Stoic elements, the dramatic fiction took priority, and that 'The ambivalence of this portrait owes more to contradictions inherent in the myth, ... than it does to Stoic categorization of the passions', *Seneca's Hercules Furens*, p. 41.

19. Billerbeck, *Seneca: Hercules Furens*.

20. On Seneca and tragedy, see Arkins, 'Heavy Seneca'; Cunliffe, *The Influence of Seneca on Elizabethan Tragedy*; Miola, *Shakespeare and Classical Tragedy*.

21. For detailed discussion of the manuscript tradition of Euripides' plays, see Turyn, *Byzantine Manuscript Tradition of the Tragedies of Euripides*; Zuntz, *An Inquiry into the Transmission of the Plays of Euripides*. The latest thinking on this issue can be found in Diggle, *The*

Textual Tradition of Euripides' Orestes, and in a more user-friendly form in Garland, *Surviving Greek Tragedy*.

22. Seznec, *La survivance des dieux antiques*.

23. See C.H. Miller, 'Hercules and his Labours as Allegories of Christ'.

24. Coluccio Salutati, *De Laboribus Herculis* (c. 1391).

25. Milton's Comus and Samson Agonistes make particular play with the Heracles myth, in addition to the famous comparison of Satan to Heracles in *Paradise Regained* 4.562-71, whereas Dante in the *Inferno* deploys Heracles as a Christ-figure. See discussion in Harding, *The Club of Heracles*.

26. See Feder, *Madness in Literature*.

27. Reid Davidson, *The Oxford Guide to Classical Mythology in the Arts 1300-1900s*. References to the madness of Heracles are on pp. 530-1.

28. Sourvinou-Inwood, *'Reading' Greek Culture*; *'Reading' Greek Death*.

29. *Hercules in New York* (1970), directed by A.A. Seidelman.

30. Lucas explicitly acknowledges his debt to world mythology via the work of Joseph Campbell, *The Hero with a Thousand Faces*.

31. Ref. http://www.members.aol.com/MG4273/herc.2.htm.

32. All page numbers taken from the 2nd edition, *The Labours of Hercules: The Legend of Poirot's Retirement* (London & Glasgow: Fontana, 1963. Original 1947).

33. p. 13.

34. p. 14.

35. p. 12.

36. See Stray, *Classics Transformed*.

37. Griffiths, 'The King and Eye'; Simon, *Tragic Drama and the Family*; Slater, *The Glory of Hera*. From a more general cultural perspective, see also Blazina, 'Mythos and Men: Towards New Paradigms of Masculinity'.

38. M. Padilla, 'Heroic Paternity in Euripides' *Herakles*'; Kraus, 'Dangerous Supplements'. The theme has also been explored by non-specialists working on myth, relating the issue to modern approaches to family dynamics; see M. Maclean, 'The Heirs of Amphitryon: Social Fathers and Natural Fathers'.

39. For a good example of the post-structuralist approach to tragedy, see Goldhill, *Reading Greek Tragedy*.

40. Dunn, 'Ends and Means'; *Tragedy's End*.

41. Worman, 'The Ties That Bind'; George, 'Euripides' *Heracles* 140-325: Staging and the Stage Iconography of Heracles' Bow'; Padilla, 'The Gorgonic Archer'; Rehm, 'Before, Behind, Beyond: Tragic Space and Euripides' *Heracles*'.

42. See the Archive's website at http://www.apgrd.ox.ac.uk. I gratefully acknowledge the help of all at the Archive, and Kathryn Riley, in researching material for this chapter.

43. U. Von Wilamowitz-Moellendorff, *Euripides: Herakles*.

44. See discussion of *Medea*'s performance history in Hall, Macintosh & Taplin, *Medea in Performance 1500-2000*.

45. Riley, 'Heracles as Dr Strangelove and GI Joe: Male Heroism Deconstructed'.

46. Armitage, *Mister Heracles*, p. 23.

47. Riley, 'Heracles as Dr Strangelove and GI Joe: Male Heroism Deconstructed', p. 141.

48. N. Loraux, 'Herakles: The Super-Male and the Feminine'.

49. Doherty, *Gender and the Interpretation of Classical Myth*.

Guide to Further Reading

Translations

W. Arrowsmith, *Heracles*, in D. Grene & R. Lattimore (editors), *The Complete Greek Tragedies. Euripides II* (Chicago: University of Chicago Press, 1952, 1956). An old translation, but still a good straightforward account of the play. Language is simple, though verse format is maintained.

J. Davie, *Euripides: Heracles and Other Plays* (London: Penguin, 2002). A powerful, modern translation with a helpful introduction to the volume. Prose format but with good line numbering.

M.R. Halleran, *The Heracles of Euripides* (Cambridge Mass.: Focus Classical Library, 1988). Provides an introduction, notes and interpretative essay to accompany the translation. Verse format.

D. Kovacs, *Euripides: Suppliant Women, Electra, Heracles* (Cambridge Mass.: Harvard University Press, Loeb Classical Library Series, 1998). Translation with facing Greek text. English stays close to the Greek original but maintains a lively, semi-poetic style.

T. Sleigh (translator), *Euripides' Herakles, Introduction and Notes by C. Wolff* (New York & Oxford: Oxford University Press, 2001). Highly readable English verse translation. Gives a good indication of the awkwardness of the dramatic structure and the density of key passages.

Commentaries and book-length studies

S.A. Barlow, *Euripides' Heracles* (Warminster: Aris and Phillips, 1996). Text with facing translation. Commentary is keyed to the translation.

G.W. Bond, *Euripides: Heracles* (Oxford: Clarendon Press, 1981). Detailed commentary on the Greek text is aimed at those reading the text in Greek, but the introduction and discussion of key scenes are valuable for all readers.

T. Papadopoulou, *Heracles and Euripidean Tragedy* (Cambridge: Cambridge University Press, forthcoming, 2005). A full study of the *Heracles*. This book was not yet published, and thus not available for full consultation, when this volume was written. It is, however, a development from Papadopoulou's doctoral thesis, *Studies in Euripides' Herakles*, to which reference is made in this volume.

U. Von Wilamowitz-Moellendorff, *Euripides: Herakles*, 3 vols (Darmstadt: Wissenschaftliche Buchgesellschaft, 1959). Still a standard reference work, containing detailed commentary on the text together with a more general discussion of aspects of the play, but not for the faint-hearted.

Heracles in Greek Myth

Detailed accounts of the sources for the mythology of Heracles can be found in Padilla, *The Myths of Herakles in Ancient Greece* (Lanham: University of America Press, 1998), and Gantz, *Early Greek Myth. A Guide to Literary and Artistic Sources* (Baltimore: Johns Hopkins University Press, 1993).

On the visual tradition, see Uhlenbrock, *Herakles: Passage of the Hero through 1000 years of Classical Art* (New Rochelle, NY; Annandale-on-Hudson, NY: A.D. Caratzas: Edith C. Blum Art Institute, Bard College, 1986); Volkommer, *Herakles in the Art of Classical Greece* (Oxford, Oxford University Committee for Archaeology Monograph No. 25, 1988).

Euripides, Heracles and Greek Tragedy

Good general introductions to Greek tragedy are provided by Sommerstein, *Greek Drama and Dramatists* (London: Routledge, 2002), and Storey & Allen, *A Guide to Ancient Greek Drama* (Oxford: Blackwell, 2005).

The evidence for the practicalities of staging and financing productions, together with evidence for all other aspects of drama, is available in English translation in E. Csapo & W.J. Slater, *The Context of Ancient Drama* (Ann Arbor: University of Michigan Press, 1994). Articles on general aspects of tragedy are found in Easterling, *The Cambridge Companion to Greek Tragedy* (Cambridge: Cambridge University Press, 1997).

On theatrical approaches to tragedy, see Taplin, *Greek Tragedy in Action* (London: Methuen, 1983), and compare the more textualist approach of Goldhill, *Reading Greek Tragedy* (Cambridge: Cambridge University Press, 1988).

Dramatic Structure and Unity

On thematic links, see Padilla, 'The Gorgonic Archer: Danger of Sight in Euripides' *Herakles*', *Classical World* 86 (1992a), pp. 1-12, on issues of vision; Worman, 'The Ties That Bind: Transformations of Costume and Connection in Euripides' *Heracles*', *Ramus* 28 (1999), pp. 89-107, on ideas of binding and yoking; and Krauss, 'Dangerous Supplements. Etymology and Genealogy in Euripides' *Heracles*', *Proceedings of the Classical Philological Society* 44 (1998), pp. 135-56, for a persuasive account of the patterns of circularity and repetition in the play.

For an opposite approach, emphasising the deliberate lack of unity, see Dunn, 'Ends and Means in Euripides' *Heracles*', in Roberts, Dunn & Fowler, *Classical Closure*, pp. 83-111.

Family Values

On the Greek family, see Pomeroy, *Families in Classical and Hellenistic Greece* (Oxford: Clarendon Press, 1997). On family dynamics in tragedy, see Simon, *Tragic Drama and the Family* (New Haven: Yale University Press, 1988), a psychoanalytical reading. For individual relationships, see Mikalson, 'Zeus the Father and Heracles the Son in Tragedy', *Transactions of the American Philological Association* 116 (1986), pp. 89-98; Griffith, 'The King and Eye: The Rule of The Father in Greek Tragedy', *Proceedings of the Cambridge Philological Society* 44 (1998), pp. 20-84.

The debate on the bow is well addressed by George, 'Euripides' *Heracles* 140-235: Staging and the Stage Iconography of Heracles' Bow', *Greek, Roman and Byzantine Studies* 35 (1994), pp. 145-57.

Violence and Madness

On madness in tragedy, see Padel, *Whom the Gods Destroy: Elements of Greek and Tragic Madness* (Princeton: Princeton University Press, 1995); Hartigan, 'Euripidean Madness: Herakles and Orestes', *Greece and Rome* 34 (1987), pp. 26-35.

On Heracles' madness in Greek literature, see Pike, 'Hercules Furens. Some Thoughts on the Madness of Heracles in Greek Literature', *Proceedings of the African Classical Associations* 14 (1978), pp. 1-6.

On hybris, see Fisher, *Hybris: A Study in the Values of Honour and Shame in Ancient Greece* (Warminster: Aris & Phillips, 1992).

Suicide and the Gods

On Heracles' 'interstitial nature', see Silk, 'Heracles and Greek Tragedy', *Greece and Rome* 32 (1985), pp. 1-22.

On divine aspects of the play, see Lawrence, 'The God that is Truly God and the Universe of Euripides' *Herakles*', *Mnemosyne* 51 (1998), pp. 127-46; Desch, 'Der *Herakles* des Euripides und die Götter', *Philologus* 130 (1986), pp. 8-23.

On suicide in general, see Garrison, *Groaning Tears. Ethical and Dramatic Aspects of Suicide in Greek Tragedy* (Leiden: Brill, 1995), and on Heracles' decision see Yoshitake, 'Disgrace, Grief and Other Ills: Heracles' Rejection of Suicide', *Journal of Hellenic Studies* 114 (1994), pp. 135-53; de Romilly, 'Le refus du suicide dans l'Héraclès d'Euripide', *Archaeognosia* 1 (1980), pp. 1-10.

Theseus and the Role of Friendship

On Theseus and Athens, see Calame, *Thésée et l'imagination Athénien. Legende et culte en Grèce antique* (Lausanne: Sciences Humaines, Editions Payot Lausanne, 1990); Mills, *Theseus, Tragedy and the Athenian Empire* (Oxford: Clarendon Press, 1997); Walker, *Theseus and Athens* (New York & Oxford: Oxford University Press, 1995).

On friendship, see Annas, 'Plato and Aristotle on Friendship and Altruism', *Mind* n.s. 86 (1977), pp. 532-54; Konstan, *Friendship in the Classical World* (Cambridge: Cambridge University Press, 1997).

After Euripides

On the Roman view of Hercules, see Shelton, *Seneca's Hercules Furens: Theme, Structure and Style* (Hypomnemata S.) (Göttingen: Vandenhoeck and Ruprecht, 1978).

For the general reception history, see Blanshard, *Hercules: Scenes from A Heroic Life* (London: Granta, 2005); K. Galinsky, *The Herakles Theme* (Oxford: Blackwell, 1972).

For the modern theatrical use of the play, see Riley, 'Heracles as Dr Strangelove and GI Joe: Male Heroism Deconstructed', in E. Hall, F. Macintosh & A. Wrigley (editors), *Dionysus Since 69. Greek Tragedy at the Dawn of the Third Millennium* (Oxford: Oxford University Press, 2004), pp. 113-142.

Bibliography

L. Abel, *Metatheatre: A New View of Dramatic Form* (New York: Hill & Wang, 1963).

H.C. Ackermann (editor), *Lexicon Iconographicum Mythologicum Classicae* (Zurich & Munich: Artemis, 1981-).

A.W.H. Adkins, 'Basic Greek Values in Euripides' *Hecuba* and *Hercules Furens*', *Classical Quarterly n.s.* 16 (1966), pp. 193-219.

G.S. Aldrete, *Gestures and Acclamations in Ancient Rome* (Baltimore & London: John Hopkins University Press, 1999).

C.F. Alford, *The Psychoanalytical Theory of Greek Tragedy* (New Haven: Yale University Press, 1992).

W. Allan, 'Euripides in Megalê Hellas. Some Aspects of the Early Reception of Tragedy', *Greece and Rome* 48 (2001), pp. 67-88.

J. Annas, 'Plato and Aristotle on Friendship and Altruism', *Mind* 86 (1977), pp. 532-4.

B. Arkins, 'Heavy Seneca. His Influence on Shakespeare', *Classics Ireland* 2.1 (1995), pp. 1-6.

S. Armitage, *Mister Heracles: After Euripides* (London: Faber & Faber, 2000).

P.D. Arnott, 'Off-Stage Cries and the Choral Presence', *Antichthon* 16 (1982), pp. 35-43.

J. Assaël, 'L'Héraclès d'Euripide et les ténèbres infernales', *Les Études Classiques* 62 (1994), pp. 313-26.

D. Auger & S. Said (editors), *Généalogies Mythiques* (Paris: Les Belles Lettres, 1998).

D. Babut, 'Xenophane's critique des poètes', *L'Antiquité Classique* 43 (1974), pp. 83-117.

D. Bain, *Masters, Servants and Orders in Greek Tragedy. A Study of Some Aspects of Dramatic Technique and Convention* (Manchester: Manchester University Press, 1981).

S.A. Barlow, *The Imagery of Euripides. A Study in the Dramatic Use of Pictorial Language* (London: Methuen, 1971).

—— 'Sophocles' *Ajax* and Euripides' *Heracles*', *Ramus* 10 (1981), pp. 115-25.

—— *Euripides: Heracles* (Warminster: Aris & Phillips, 1996).

C. Barone, 'L'apaidia in Euripide: terminologia specifica', *Materiali e discussion per l'analisi dei testi classici* 18 (1976), pp. 57-67.

Bibliography

M.J. Bataille, 'Le *fou* et le devin dans la tragédie grecque', in Ghiron-Bistagne, *Transe et Théâtre*, Actes de la table ronde internationale Montpellier 3-5 mars 1988. Textes réunis par Ghiron-Bistagne Paulette, Cahiers du GITA 4 (Montpellier: Université/ Montpellier, 1988), pp. 147-56.

E. Belfiore, *Murder Among Friends. Violation of Philia in Greek Tragedy* (New York & Oxford: Oxford University Press, 2000).

V. Berg, 'Alcestis and Hercules in the catacomb of Via Latina', *Vigilae Christianae* 48.3 (1994), pp. 219-34.

M. Bernal, *Black Athena. The Afroasiatic Roots of Classical Civilisation* (London: Vintage Books, 1987).

V. Bers, *Speech in Speech. Studies in Incorporated Oratio Recta in Attic Drama and Oratory* (Lanham, Boulder, New York & London: Rowman and Littlefield Publishers Inc., 1997).

S. Bertman (editor), *The Conflict of Generations in Ancient Greece and Rome* (Amsterdam: Gruner, 1976).

S. Beta, 'Madness on the Comic Stage', *Greek, Roman and Byzantine Studies* 40 (1999), pp. 135-58.

J.H. Betts, J.T. Hooker & J. Green (editors), *Studies in Honour of T.B.L. Webster* (Bristol: Bristol Classical Press, 1986).

M. Billerbeck, *Seneca: Hercules Furens* (Leiden: Brill, 1999).

G. Binder, 'Hercules und Claudius', *Rheinisches Museum* 117 (1974), pp. 288-317.

J. Bingen, G. Cambier & G. Nachtergael (editors), *Le monde grec: hommages à Claire Préaux* (Brussels: Université de Bruxelles, 1975).

A. Blanshard, *Hercules: Scenes from A Heroic Life* (London: Granta, 2005).

C. Blazina, 'Mythos and Men: Towards New Paradigms of Masculinity', *Journal of Men's Studies* 5.4 (1997), pp. 285-99.

M.W. Blundell, *Helping Friends and Harming Enemies* (Cambridge: Cambridge University Press, 1989).

J. Boardman, 'Herakles in Extremis', in Böhr & Martini, *Studien zur Mythologie*, pp. 127-32.

——— 'Herakles, Peisistratos and Eleusis', *Journal of Hellenic Studies* 95 (1975), pp. 1-12.

——— 'Herakles, Peisistratos, and the Unconvinced', *Journal of Hellenic Studies* 109 (1989), pp. 158-9.

D. Boedeker, 'Becoming Medea. Assimilation in Euripides', in Clauss & Johnston, *Medea*, pp. 127-48.

A. Boeghold, 'Perikles' Citizenship Law of 451/0 BC', in Boegehold & Scafuro, *Athenian Identity and Civic Ideology*, pp. 57-66.

A. Boeghold & A. Scafuro (editors), *Athenian Identity and Civic Ideology* (Baltimore: Johns Hopkins University Press, 1994).

E. Böhr & W. Martini (editors), *Studien zur Mythologie und Vasenmalerei* (Mainz: P. von Zabern, 1986).

Bibliography

G.W. Bond, 'Euripidean Parody of Aeschylus', *Hermathena* 118 (1974), pp. 1-14.

—— *Euripides: Heracles* (Oxford: Clarendon Press, 1981).

C. Bonnét, *MELQART: Cultes et mythes de l'Héraclès Tyrien en méditerranée* (Namur: Studia Phoenicia VIII, 1988).

C. Bonnét & C. Jourdain-Annequin (editors), *Héraclès: d'une rive à l'autre de la méditerranée. Bilan et perspectives* (Brussels & Rome: Institut historique belge de Rome, 1992).

E.K. Borthwick (1990), 'Bees and Drones in Aristotle, Aelian and Euripides', *Bulletin of the Institute of Classical Studies* 37 (1990), pp. 57-62.

D. Boulogne, 'Les doubles paternités, le cas de Thésée', in Auger & Said, *Généalogies Mythiques*, pp. 212-43.

A. Bowie, *Aristophanes. Myth, Ritual and Comedy* (Cambridge: Cambridge University Press, 1994).

L. Bowman (1999), 'Prophecy and Authority in the *Trachiniae*', *American Journal of Philology* 120 (1999), pp. 335-50.

A.J. Boyle, *Tragic Seneca: An Essay in the Theatrical Tradition* (London: Routledge, 1997).

G. Boys-Stones, *Post Hellenistic Philosophy* (Oxford: Oxford University Press, 2001).

C. Brillante, 'La paideia di Eracle', in Bonnét & Jourdain-Annequin, *Héraclès: d'une rive à l'autre de la méditerranée. Bilan et perspectives*, pp. 199-222.

F. Budelmann & P. Michelakis (editors), *Homer, Tragedy and Beyond. Essays in Honour of P.E. Easterling* (London: Society for the Promotion of Hellenic Studies, 2001).

W. Burkert, 'Le mythe de Géryon', in Gentili & Paioni, *Il Mito Greco*, pp. 273-84.

—— *Greek Religion: Archaic and Classical* (Oxford: Blackwell, 1985).

A. Burnett, *Catastrophe Survived: Euripides' Plays of Mixed Reversal* (Oxford: Oxford University Press, 1971).

R.G.A. Buxton, *Sophocles* (Oxford: Oxford University Press, 1984).

—— *Sophocles* (Oxford: Oxford University Press, 1984). 'Euripides' Alcestis: Five Aspects of An Interpretation', *Dodoni Philologia Tomos* 1 (1985), pp. 75-89.

—— *Imaginary Greece. The Contexts of Mythology* (Cambridge: Cambridge University Press, 1994).

—— *The Complete World of Greek Mythology* (London: Thames & Hudson, 2004).

S. Byl, 'Lamentations sur la vieillesse dans la tragédie grecque', in Bingen, Cambier & Nachtergael, *Le monde grec*, pp. 130-9.

E. Cahan, J. Mechling, B. Sutton-Smith & S.H. White, 'The Elusive Historical Child: Ways of Knowing the Child of History and

Psychology', in Elder Jr., Modell & Parke, *Children in Time and Place. Developmental and Historical Insights*, pp.192-223.

C. Calame, *Thésée et l'imagination Athénien. Legende et culte en Grèce antique* (Lausanne: Sciences Humaines, Editions Payot Lausanne, 1990).

J. Campbell, *The Hero with a Thousand Faces* (Princeton: Princeton University Press, 1968).

T.H. Carpenter, *Art and Myth in Ancient Greece* (London: Thames and Hudson, 1991).

J. Carrière, 'L'Apparition d'Athéna dans l'Héraclès d'Euripide', C. Crimi *et al.*, *Studi Classici in Onore di Quintino Cataudella* vol. 1 (1972), pp. 233-6.

H.H.O. Chalk, 'ARETH and BIA in Euripides' *Herakles*', *Journal of Hellenic Studies* 82 (1962), pp. 7-18.

G. Chancellor, 'Implicit Stage Directions in Ancient Greek Drama: Critical Assumptions and the Reading Public', *Arethusa* 12 (1979), pp. 133-52.

J.J. Clauss & S.I. Johnston (editors), *Medea: Essays on Medea in Myth, Literature, Philosophy and Art* (Princeton: University of Princeton Press, 1997).

D. Cohen, *Law, Violence and Community in Classical Athens* (Cambridge: Cambridge University Press, 1995).

S.G. Cole (1984), 'The Social Function of Rituals of Maturation: The Koureion and the Arkteia', *Zeitschrift für Papyrologie und Epigraphik* 55 (1984), pp. 233-44.

C.M. Collard, M. Cropp & K.H. Lee, *Euripides: Selected Fragmentary Plays I* (Warminster: Aris & Phillips, 1995).

N.E. Collinge, 'Medical Terms and Clinical Attitudes in the Tragedians', *Bulletin of the Institute of Classical Studies* 9 (1962), pp. 43-55.

D.J. Conacher, 'Theme, Plot and Technique in the *Heracles* of Euripides', *Phoenix* 9 (1955), pp. 139-52.

―――― *Aeschylus: Prometheus Bound. A Literary Commentary* (Toronto: University of Toronto Press, 1996).

―――― *Aeschylus. The Earlier Plays and Related Studies* (Toronto: University of Toronto Press, 1996).

W.R. Connor, 'Theseus and His City', in Hellstrom & Alroth, *Religion and Power in the Ancient Greek World*, pp. 115-20.

M.J. Cropp, *A Stylistic and Analytical Commentary on Euripides' Herakles 1-814* (Toronto: Diss. Phil. University of Toronto, 1976).

M.J. Cropp & G. Fick, *Resolutions and Chronology in Euripides: The Fragmentary Tragedies*, Supplement 43 of *Bulletin of the Institute of Classical Studies* (London: Institute of Classical Studies, 1985).

M.J. Cropp & K.H. Lee (editors), *Euripides and Tragic Theatre in the*

Late 5th Century (Champaign: Stipes Publishing, 2000. *Illinois Classical Studies* 24/25).

E. Csapo & W.J. Slater, *The Context of Ancient Drama* (Ann Arbor: University of Michigan Press, 1994).

J.W. Cunliffe, *The Influence of Seneca on Elizabethan Tragedy* (London: Archon Books, 1965).

C. Cusset, 'L'enfance perdue d'Héraclès: l'image du héros au service de l'autre', *Bulletin de l'Association Guillaume Budé* (1999), pp. 191-210.

L. Danforth, *The Death Rituals of Rural Greece* (Princeton: Princeton University Press 1982).

J. Reid Davidson, *The Oxford Guide to Classical Mythology in the Arts 1300-1900s* (Oxford: Oxford University Press, 1993).

J. Davie, *Euripides: Heracles and other Plays* (London: Penguin, 2002).

S. Deacy & A. Villings (editors), *Athena in the Classical World* (Leiden: Brill, 2001).

N. Demand, *Birth, Death and Motherhood in Classical Greece* (Baltimore: Johns Hopkins University Press, 1994).

W. Desch, 'Der *Herakles* des Euripides und die Götter', *Philologus* 130 (1986), pp. 8-23.

M. Detienne & J.-P. Vernant (editors), *The Cuisine of Sacrifice among the Greeks* (Chicago: University of Chicago Press, 1989. Original, Paris 1979).

G. Devereux, 'The Self-Blinding of Oedipus', *Journal of Hellenic Studies* 93 (1973), pp. 31-49.

J. Diggle, *The Textual Tradition of Euripides' Orestes* (Oxford: Clarendon Press, 1991).

G. Dobrov, *Figures of Play. Greek Drama and Metafictional Poetics* (Oxford: Oxford University Press, 2001).

L.E. Doherty, *Gender and the Interpretation of Classical Myth* (London: Duckworth, 2001).

K. Dowden, *The Uses of Greek Mythology* (London: Routledge, 1992).

J. Duchemin, 'Le personage de Lyssa dans *L'Héraclès Furieux* d'Euripide', *Révue des Études Grecques* 80 (1967), pp. 130-9.

J.-R. Dumanior, 'La moisson d'Héraclès: le héros, le domaine et les enfants dans Les Trachiniennes', *Révue des Études Grecques* 109 (1996), pp. 381-409.

G. Dumézil, *The Destiny of a King*, translated by A. Hiltebeitel (Chicago: University of Chicago Press, 1971).

F.M. Dunn, 'Euripides and the Rites of Hera Akraia', *Greek, Roman and Byzantine Studies* 35 (1994), pp. 103-15.

—— *Tragedy's End. Closure and Innovation in Euripidean Drama* (New York & Oxford: Oxford University Press, 1996).

—— 'Ends and Means in Euripides' *Heracles*', in Roberts, Dunn & Fowler, *Classical Closure*, pp. 83-111.

Bibliography

M. Dyson (1988), 'Alcestis' Children and the Character of Admetus', *Journal of Hellenic Studies* 108 (1988), pp. 13-23.

M. Dyson & K.H. Lee, 'The Funeral of Astyanax in Euripides' *Troades*', *Journal of Hellenic Studies* 120 (2000), pp. 17-33.

P.E. Easterling, 'Constructing The Heroic', in Pelling, *Greek Tragedy and the Historian*, pp. 21-38.

—— 'The Tragic Homer', *Bulletin of the Institute of Classical Studies* 31 (1984), pp. 1-8.

—— (editor), *The Cambridge Companion to Greek Tragedy* (Cambridge: Cambridge University Press, 1997).

—— 'From Repertoire to Canon', in *The Cambridge Companion to Greek Tragedy*, pp. 211-27.

P.E. Easterling & E. Hall (editors), *Greek and Roman Actors* (Cambridge: Cambridge University Press, 2002).

M. Ebbott, *Imagining Illegitimacy. Illegitimacy in Classical Greek Literature* (Lanham, MD: Lexington Books, 2003).

G.H. Elder Jr., J. Modell & R.H. Parke, *Children in Time and Place. Developmental and Historical Insights* (New York: Cambridge University Press, 1993).

M. Erasmo, *Roman Tragedy. Theatre to Theatricality* (Austin: University of Texas, 2004).

T.M. Falkner, 'Euripides and the Stagecraft of Old Age', in Hartigan, *The Many Forms of Drama*, pp. 41-50.

P. Fedeli, 'Ideologia augustea e poesia: il mito di Ercole e Caco in Properzio', in Rosen, *Macht und Kultur im Rom der Kaiserzeit*, pp. 109-19.

L. Feder, *Madness in Literature* (Princeton: Princeton University Press, 1980).

E. Filhol, 'Herakleié nosos. L'épilepsie d'Héraclès', *Révue d'Histoire de Religions* 206 (1989), pp. 3-20.

N.R.E. Fisher, *Hybris: A Study in the Values of Honour and Shame in Ancient Greece* (Warminster: Aris & Phillips, 1992).

J.G. Fitch, *Seneca's Hercules Furens* (Ithaca: Cornell University Press, 1987).

G.T. Fitzgerald, 'The Euripidean Heracles. An Intellectual and a Coward', *Mnemosyne* 54 (1991), pp. 85-95.

H. Foley, *Ritual Irony: Poetry and Sacrifice in Euripides* (Ithaca: Cornell University Press, 1985).

—— 'Choral Identity in Greek Tragedy', *Classical Philology* 98 (2003), pp. 1-30.

A. Ford, *Homer: The Poetry of the Past* (Ithaca: Cornell University Press, 1992).

W.G. Forrest, 'An Athenian Generation Gap', *Yale Classical Studies* 24 (1975), pp. 37-52.

R.L. Fowler, 'Genealogical Thinking. Hesiod's Catalogue and the

Creation of the Hellenes', *Proceedings of the Cambridge Philological Society* 44 (1998), pp. 1-19.

—— (editor), *The Cambridge Companion to Homer* (Cambridge Companions to Literature) (Cambridge: Cambridge University Press, 2004).

E. Franzino, 'Euripides' *Heracles* 858-73', *Illinois Classical Studies* 20 (1995), pp. 57-63.

W.D. Furley, *Studies in the Use of Fire in Ancient Greek Religion* (Salem: Ayer, 1981).

——'Euripides on the Sanity of Heracles', in Betts, Hooker & Green, *Studies in Honour of T.B.L. Webster*, pp. 102-13.

M. Gagarin, 'Dike in Archaic Greek Thought', *Classical Philology* 69 (1974), pp. 186-97.

K. Galinsky, *The Herakles Theme* (Oxford: Blackwell, 1972).

T. Gantz, *Early Greek Myth. A Guide to Literary and Artistic Sources* (Baltimore: Johns Hopkins University Press, 1993).

R. Garland, *The Greek Way of Death* (Ithaca: Cornell University Press, 1985).

—— *The Greek Way of Life From Conception to Old Age* (Ithaca: Cornell University Press, 1990).

—— *Surviving Greek Tragedy* (London: Duckworth, 2004).

R. Garner, *From Homer to Tragedy. The Art of Allusion in Greek Poetry* (London: Routledge, 1984).

E.P. Garrison, *Groaning Tears. Ethical and Dramatic Aspects of Suicide in Greek Tragedy* (Leiden: Brill, 1995).

M. Gellrich, 'Interpreting Greek Tragedy. History, Theory, and the New Philology', in Goff, *History, Tragedy, Theory*, pp. 38-58.

B. Gentili & G. Paioni (editors), *Il Mito Greco* (Rome: QUCC. dell'Ateneo e Bizzarri, 1977).

D.B. George, 'Euripides' *Heracles* 140-235: Staging and the Stage Iconography of Heracles' Bow', *Greek, Roman and Byzantine Studies* 35 (1994), pp. 145-57.

J. Gibert, 'Euripides' *Heracles* 1351 and the Hero's Encounter with Death', *Classical Philology* 92 (1997), pp. 247-57.

René Girard, *Mensonge romantique et vérité romanesque* (Paris, 1961); in English *Deceit, Desire and the Novel*, translated by Yvonne Freccero (Baltimore: Johns Hopkins University Press, 1965).

——*The Theater of Envy: William Shakespeare* (New York: Oxford University Press, 1991).

B. Goff (editor), *History, Tragedy, Theory. Dialogues on Athenian Drama* (Austin: University of Texas Press, 1995).

H. Golder, 'Making a Scene: Gesture, Tableaux and the Tragic Chorus', *Arion* 3rd series 4.1 (1996), pp. 1-19.

B.E. Goldfarb, 'The Conflict of Obligations in Euripides' *Alcestis*', *Greek, Roman and Byzantine Studies* 33 (1992), pp. 109-26.

S. Goldhill, *Reading Greek Tragedy* (Cambridge: Cambridge University Press, 1988).

—— 'The Great Dionysia and Civic Ideology', in Winkler & Zeitlin, *Nothing To Do With Dionysos?*, pp. 97-129.

—— 'The Audience of Greek Tragedy', in Easterling *The Cambridge Companion to Greek Tragedy*, pp. 54-68.

S. Goldhill & R. Osborne (editors), *Performance Culture and Athenian Democracy* (Cambridge: Cambridge University Press, 1999).

R.L. Gordon, 'Reason and Ritual in Greek Tragedy: On Rene Girard, Violence and the Sacred', *Comparative Criticism Yearbook* 1 (Cambridge: Cambridge University Press, 1979), pp. 279-310.

B. Goward, *Telling Tragedy. Narrative Technique in Aeschylus, Sophocles and Euripides* (London: Duckworth, 1999).

C. Goyens-Slezakowa, 'L'initiation dans le Philoctète de Sophocle', in Moreau, *L'initiation*, pp. 135-52.

J.W. Gregory, 'Euripides' Heracles', in T.F. Gould & C.J. Herington, *Greek Tragedy*, Yale Classical Studies 25 (Cambridge: Cambridge University Press, 1977), pp. 259-76.

J. Griffin, 'The Social Function of Attic Tragedy', *Classical Quarterly* 48 (1998), pp. 39-61.

M. Griffith, *The Authenticity of Prometheus Bound* (Cambridge: Cambridge University Press, 1977).

—— 'The King and Eye: The Rule of the Father in Greek Tragedy', *Proceedings of the Cambridge Philological Society* 44 (1998), pp. 20-84.

—— 'Slaves of Dionysos: Satyrs, Audience and the Ends of the *Oresteia*', *Classical Antiquity* 21.2 (2002), pp. 195-258.

E.M. Griffiths, 'Euripides' *Herakles* and the Pursuit of Immortality', *Mnemosyne* 55 (2002), pp. 641-56.

M.D. Grmek, 'Ideas on Heredity in Greek and Roman Antiquity', *Physis n.s.* 28 (1991), pp. 11-34.

W.W. Grummond, 'Heracles' Entrance: An Illustration of Euripidean Method', *Eranos* 52 (1983), pp. 83-90.

E. Hall, 'The Sociology of Athenian Tragedy', in Easterling, *The Cambridge Companion to Greek Tragedy*, pp. 93-126.

E. Hall, F. Macintosh & O. Taplin (editors), *Medea in Performance 1500-2000* (Oxford: Legenda, 2000).

E. Hall, F. Macintosh & A. Wrigley (editors), *Dionysus since 69: Greek Tragedy at the Dawn of the Third Millennium* (Oxford: Oxford University Press, 2004).

M.R. Halleran, *Stagecraft in Euripides* (London: Croom Helm, 1985).

—— 'Rhetoric, Irony and the Ending of Euripides' *Herakles*', *Classical Antiquity* 5 (1986), pp. 171-81.

J.P. Hallett & T. Van Nortwick (editors), *Compromising Traditions: The Personal Voice in Classical Scholarship* (London & New York: Routledge, 1993).

Bibliography

D.M. Halperin, J.J. Winkler & F.I. Zeitlin (editors), *Before Sexuality*: *The Construction of Erotic Experience in the Ancient World* (Princeton: Princeton University Press, 1990), pp. 21-52.

R. Hamilton, 'Cries Within and the Tragic Skene', *American Journal of Philology* 108 (1987), pp. 585-99.

—— 'Slings and Arrows: The Debate with Lycus in the *Heracles*', *Transactions of the American Philological Association* 115 (1988), pp. 19-125.

E.W. Handley, 'Aristophanes and the Athenian Generation Gap', *Yale Classical Studies* 24 (1975), pp. 37-52.

J. Hangard, 'Remarques sur quelques motifs répétés dans l'*Héraclès* d'Euripide', in Bremer, Radt & Ruijgh, *Miscellanea Tragica in Honorem J.C. Kamerbeek*, pp. 125-46.

W. Hansen, *Ariadne's Thread*: *A Guide to International Tales Found in Classical Literature* (Ithaca & London: Cornell University Press, 2002).

D.P. Harding, *The Club of Heracles. Studies in the Classical Background to Paradise Lost* (Urbana: University of Illinois Press, 1962).

K. Hartigan, 'Euripidean Madness: Herakles and Orestes', *Greece and Rome* 34 (1987), pp. 26-35.

—— (editor), *The Many Forms of Drama* (Lanham, MD: University Press of America, 1985).

J. Haubold, 'Epic with an End: An Interpretation of Homeric Hymns 15 and 20', in Budelmann & Michelakis, *Homer, Tragedy and Beyond*, pp. 23-41.

G. Havelock, 'The Oral Composition of Greek Drama', in G. Havelock, *The Literate Revolution* (Princeton: Princeton University Press, 1982).

R. Hawley & B. Levick (editors), *Women in Antiquity. New Assessments* (New York: Routledge, 1995).

P. Hellstrom & B. Alroth (editors), *Religion and Power in the Ancient Greek World* (Uppsala: Proceedings of the Uppsala Symposium, 1996).

J.P. Hesk, *Ajax* (London: Duckworth, 2003).

O. Hesker, *Commodus*: *An Emperor at the Crossroads* (Amsterdam: J.C. Gießen, 2002).

W.E. Higgins, 'Deciphering Time in the Herakles of Euripides', *Quaderni urbinati di cultura classica* 47 (1984), pp. 89-109.

P. Holt, 'Herakles' Apotheosis in Lost Greek Literature and Art', *L'Antiquité Classique* 61 (1992), pp. 15-46.

J.T. Hooker, *The Ancient Spartans* (London: J.M. Dent, 1980).

S. Hornblower, *The Greek World 479-323 BC*, rev. ed. (London: Routledge, 1991).

R.F.C. Hull, *The Archetypes and the Collective Unconscious* (London: Routledge, 1991).

Bibliography

R.L. Hunter, *Apollonius of Rhodes: The Golden Fleece* (Oxford: Oxford University Press, 1993).

M. Huys, 'EKYESIS and APOYESIS. The Terminology of Infant Exposure in Greek Antiquity', *L'Antiquité Classique* 5 (1989), pp. 190-7.

—— 'Euripides' *Auge* Fr. 265, 272, 278, 864N and the Role of Herakles in the Play', *SEJG (Sacris Erudiri)* 31 (1989-90), pp. 169-85.

—— *The Tale of the Hero who was Exposed at Birth in Euripidean Tragedy* (Leuven: Leuven University Press, 1995).

—— 'The Spartan Practice of Selective Infanticide and its Parallels in Ancient Utopian Tradition', Ancient Society 27 (1996), pp. 47-74.

W. Jaeger, *Paideia*, 3 vols (Oxford: Blackwell, 1933-43).

—— 'The Greek Idea of Immortality', *Harvard Theological Review* 52 (1959), pp. 135-47.

M. Jameson, *Sophocles: Trachiniae* (Chicago: University of Chicago Press, 1957).

M.W. Janan, 'Refashioning Hercules. Propertius 4.9', *Helios* 25 (1998), pp. 65-77.

I. de Jong, *Narrative in Drama: The Art of the Euripidean Messenger Speech* (Leiden: Brill, 1991).

F. Jouan, *Mort et fecondité dans les mythologies* (Paris: Les Belles Lettres, 1986).

C. Jourdain-Annequin, *Héraclès aux portes du soir: mythe et histoire* (Paris: Les Belles Lettres, 1989).

—— 'A propos d'un rituel pour Iolaos à Agyrion. Héraclès et l'initation des jeunes gens', in Moreau, *L'initiation. Tome I*, pp. 121-41.

C. Jourdain-Annequin & C. Bonnét (editors), *Héraclès: les femmes et le feminin: IIe rencontre héracléenne* (Brussels: Institut Historique Belge de Rome, 1996).

R. Just, *Women in Athenian Law and Life* (London: Routledge, 1989).

D. Kagan, 'The Origins and Purpose of Ostracism', *Hesperia* 30 (1961), pp. 393-402.

J.C. Kamerbeek, 'Unity and Meaning in Euripides' *Heracles*', *Mnemosyne* 39 (1966), pp. 1-16.

E. Kearns, *The Heroes of Attica*, Supplement 47 of the *Bulletin of the Institute of Classical Studies* (London: Institute of Classical Studies, 1989).

H. King, *Hippocrates' Woman* (London & New York: Routledge, 1998).

G.S. Kirk, 'Methodological Reflexions on the Myths of Herakles', in Gentili & Paioni, *Il Mito Greco*, pp. 285-97.

D. Konstan, 'An Anthropology of Euripides' *Kyklops*', in Winkler and Zeitlin, *Nothing to do with Dionysos?*, pp. 207-27.

—— 'Greek Friendship', *American Journal of Philology* 117 (1996), pp. 71-94.

Bibliography

———— *Friendship in the Classical World* (Cambridge: Cambridge University Press, 1997).

J. Kosak, *Heroic Measures. Hippocratic Medicine in the Making of Euripidean Tragedy* (Leiden: Brill, 2004).

D. Kovacs, *Euripides: Suppliant Women, Electra, Heracles* (Cambridge, Mass.: Harvard University Press, 1998).

C.S. Krauss, 'Dangerous Supplements. Etymology and Genealogy in Euripides' *Heracles*', *Proceedings of the Classical Philological Society* 44 (1998), pp. 135-56.

M. Kuntz, 'The Prodikean Choice of Herakles', *Classical Journal* 89 (1994), pp. 163-81.

W.K. Lacey, *The Family in Classical Greece* (Ithaca: Cornell University Press, 1968).

I. Lada-Richards, *Initiating Dionysus. Ritual and Theatre in Aristophanes' Frogs* (Oxford: Oxford University Press, 1999a).

———— 'Staging the Ephebeia: Theatrical Role-Playing and Ritual Transition in Sophocles' *Philoctetes*', *Ramus* 27 (1999b), pp. 1-26.

R. Lane Fox, *Alexander the Great* (Harmondsworth: Penguin, 1994).

A.-F. Laurens (editor), *Entre hommes et dieux: le convive, le héros, le prophète* (Paris: Les Belles Lettres, 1998).

S.E. Lawrence, 'The God that is Truly God and the Universe of Euripides' *Heracles*', *Mnemosyne* 51 (1998), pp. 127-46.

K.H. Lee, 'The Iris–Lyssa Scene in Euripides' *Heracles*', *Antichthon* 16 (1982), pp. 44-3.

M. Lefkowitz, 'Impiety in Euripides', *Classical Quarterly n.s.* 39 (1989), pp. 70-89.

J.H. Lesher, *Xenophanes of Colophon: Fragments. A Text and Translation with Commentary* (Toronto: University of Toronto Press, 2002).

P. Lévêque & J. Verbanck-Piérard, 'Héraclès héros ou dieu?', in *Héraclès d'une rive à l'autre de la méditerrannée. Bilan et perspectives* (Brussels: Université de Bruxelles, 1992), pp. 43-65.

H. Lloyd-Jones, 'Herakles at Eleusis: P. Oxy 2622 and P.S.I. 1391', *Maia* 19 (1967), pp. 206-9.

S. Lombardo (translator), *Homer: Iliad* (Indianapolis: Hackett, 1997).

N. Loraux, *The Invention of Athens: The Funeral Oration in the Classical City* (Cambridge, Mass: Harvard University Press, 1986).

———— *Tragic Ways of Killing a Woman* (Cambridge, Mass: Harvard University Press, 1987).

———— *The Experience of Tiresias: The Feminine and the Greek Man*, translated by Paula Wissing (Princeton: Princeton University Press, 1997).

———— 'Herakles: The Super-Male and the Feminine', in Halperin, Winkler & Zeitlin, *Before Sexuality*, pp. 21-52.

Bibliography

M. Maclean, 'The Heirs of Amphitryon: Social Fathers and Natural Fathers', *New Literary History* 26.4 (1995), pp. 787-807.

C.W. Macleod, 'Clothing in the *Oresteia*', *Maia* 27 (1975), pp. 201-3.

J. Maitland, 'Dynasty and Family in the Athenian City-State: A View from Attic Tragedy', *Classical Quarterly n.s.* 42 (1992), pp. 26-40.

C.W. Marshall, 'The Children of Heracles in *The Children of Heracles*', *Text and Presentation* 19 (1999), pp. 80-90.

—— 'Some Fifth Century Masking Conventions', *Greece and Rome* 46 (1999), pp. 188-202.

—— '*Alcestis* and the Problem of Prosatyric Drama', *Classical Journal* 95 (2000), pp. 229-38.

S. Mathé, 'Les enfants de Chiron', in Auger, *Généalogies Mythiques*, pp. 45-62.

M. Mathieu, 'Résurrection et immortalisation', in Jouan, *Mort et fécondite dans les mythologies*, pp. 39-49.

C. Martindale, *Redeeming the Text* (Cambridge: Cambridge University Press, 1993).

—— 'Proper Voices: Writing the Writer', in Hallett & Van Nortwick, *Compromising Traditions*, pp. 73-101.

F. De Martino & A.H. Sommerstein (editors), *Lo spettacolo delle voci* (Bari: Levante, 1995).

L. McClure, 'Female Speech and Characterization in Euripides', in De Martino & Sommerstein, *Lo spettacolo delle voci*, pp. 35-60.

M. Menu, 'L'enfant chez Euripide: affectivité et dramaturgie', *Pallas* 38 (1992) pp. 239-58.

R. Meridor, 'Plot and Myth in Euripides' *Heracles* and *Troades*', *Phoenix* 38 (1984), pp. 205-15.

A.N. Michelini, *Euripides and the Tragic Tradition* (Madison: University of Wisconsin Press, 1987).

J.D. Mikalson, 'Zeus the Father and Heracles the Son in Tragedy', *Transactions of the American Philological Association* 116 (1986), pp. 89-98.

—— *Honour Thy Gods: Popular Religion in Greek Tragedy* (Chapel Hill: University of North Carolina Press, 1991).

C.H. Miller, 'Hercules and his Labours as Allegories of Christ and His Victory over Sin in Dante's *Inferno*', *Quaderni d'Italianistica* 5.1 (1984), pp. 1-17.

P. Millett, *Lending and Borrowing in Ancient Athens* (Cambridge: Cambridge University Press, 1991).

H. Mills (1984), 'Greek Clothing Regulations – Sacred or Profane', *Zeitschrift für Papyrologie und Epigraphik* 55 (1984), pp. 255-65.

S. Mills, *Theseus, Tragedy and the Athenian Empire* (Oxford: Clarendon Press, 1997).

R.S. Miola, *Shakespeare and Classical Tragedy: The Influence of Seneca* (Oxford: Clarendon Press, 1992).

D.G. Mitten, J.G. Pedly & J. Ayer Scott (editors), *Studies Presented to George M.A. Hanfmann* (Mainz: Verlag P. von Zabern, 1971).

M.B. Moore, 'Athena and Herakles on Exekias' Calyx Krater', *American Journal of Archaeology* 90 (1986), pp. 35-9.

A. Moreau (editor), *L'initiation. Actes du Colloque International de Montpellier 11-14 Avril 1991* (Montpellier: Université Paul Valery, 1992).

C.H. Morgan, 'The Sculptures of the Hephaisteion', *Hesperia* 31 (1962), pp. 210-35.

A. Motte, 'Le thème des enfances divines dans le mythe grec', *Les Études Classiques* 64 (1996), pp. 109-25.

C. Moussy, 'Recherches sur *trophos*: les verbes grecs signifiant nourrir', *Études et Commentaires* LXX (Paris: Klincksieck, 1969).

F. Muecke, 'I Know You by Your Rages. Costume and Disguise in Fifth Century Drama', *Antichthon* 16 (1982), pp. 17-34.

H.G. Mullens, 'Hercules Furens and Aeschylus', *Classical Review* 53 (1939), pp. 165-6.

G. Murray, *Greek Studies* (Oxford: Clarendon Press, 1946).

G. Nagy, *Homeric Responses* (Austin: University of Texas Press, 2004).

J. Neils, 'Athena. Alter Ego of Zeus', in Deacy & Villings, *Athena in the Classical World*, pp. 219-32.

D. Ogden, *Greek Bastardy in the Classical and Hellenistic Periods* (Oxford: Clarendon Press, 1996).

C. Orwin, *The Humanity of Thucydides* (Princeton: Princeton University Press, 1994).

R. Osborne & S. Hornblower (editors), *Ritual, Finance, Politics. Athenian Democratic Accounts Presented to David Lewis* (Oxford: Clarendon Press, 1994).

C. Pache, *Baby and Child Heroes in Ancient Greece* (Urbana: University of Illinois Press, 2004).

R. Padel, 'Making Space Speak', in Winkler & Zeitlin, *Nothing to do with Dionysos?*, pp. 336-65.

—— *In and Out of the Mind* (Princeton: Princeton University Press, 1992).

—— *Whom the Gods Destroy: Elements of Greek and Tragic Madness* (Princeton: Princeton University Press, 1995).

M. Padilla, 'The Gorgonic Archer: Danger of Sight in Euripides' *Herakles*', *Classical World* 86 (1992a), pp. 1-12.

—— 'The Heraclean Dionysus: Theatrical and Social Renewal in Aristophanes' *Frogs*', *Arethusa* 25.3 (1992b), pp. 359-84.

—— 'Heroic Paternity in Euripides' *Herakles*', *Arethusa* 27 (1994), pp. 279-302.

—— *The Myths of Herakles in Ancient Greece* (Lanham: University of America Press, 1998).

T. Papadopoulou, *Studies in Euripides' Herakles* (Cambridge:

Diss. Phil. 1999), developed into *Heracles and Euripidean Tragedy* (Cambridge: Cambridge University Press, forthcoming 2005).

—— 'Herakles and Hercules. The Hero's Ambivalence in Euripides and Seneca', *Mnemosyne* 57 (2004), pp. 257-83.

—— 'Representations of Athena in Greek Tragedy', in Deacy & Villings, *Athena in the Classical World*, pp. 293-310.

E. Paratore, *Il prologo dello Hercules furens di Seneca e l'Eracle di Euripide* (Rome: Edizione dell'Ateneo, 1966. Quaderni della Rivista di cultura classica e medioevale, 9).

J. Park Poe, *Heroism and Divine Justice* (Leiden: Brill, 1974).

R. Parker, *Miasma: Pollution and Purification in Early Greek Religion*, 2nd ed. (Oxford: Clarendon Press, 1996).

—— 'Gods Cruel and Kind: Tragedy and Civic Theology', in Pelling, *Greek Tragedy and the Historian*, pp. 143-60.

H. Parry, 'The Second Stasimon of Euripides' *Heracles'*, *American Journal of Philology* 86 (1965), pp. 363-74.

C.B. Patterson, *Pericles' Citizenship Law of 451-50 BC* (New York: Arno Press, 1981).

—— *The Family in Greek History* (Cambridge, Mass.: Harvard University Press, 1998).

B. Patzek, *Homer und seine Zeit* (Munich: Verlag C.H. Beck, 2003).

E. Pechstein, *Euripides Satyrographus* (Stuttgart & Leipzig: Teubner, 1998).

C. Pelling (editor), *Characterization and Individuality in Greek Literature* (Oxford: Oxford University Press, 1990).

—— (editor), *Greek Tragedy and the Historian* (Oxford: Oxford University Press, 1997).

E. Pellizer, 'Figures narrative de la mort et l'immortalité. Sisyphe et autres histoires', *Metis* 4 (1989), pp. 269-90.

D.L. Pike, 'Hercules Furens. Some Thoughts on the Madness of Heracles in Greek Literature', *Proceedings of the African Classical Associations* 14 (1978), pp. 1-6.

—— 'Pindar's Treatment of the Heracles Myths', *Acta* 27 (1984), pp. 15-22.

A.J. Podlecki, 'Could Women Attend the Theater in Ancient Athens?', *Ancient World* 21 (1990), pp. 27-43.

S.B. Pomeroy, *Goddesses, Whores, Wives and Slaves* (New York: Schocken Books, 1975).

—— *Families in Classical and Hellenistic Greece* (Oxford: Clarendon Press, 1997).

D. Porter, *Only Connect. Three Studies in Greek Tragedy* (Lanham, MD: United Press of America, 1987).

H. Pournara-Karydas, *The 'Trophos' from Homer to Euripides as a Figure of Authority* (Seattle: Dissertation, University of Washington, 1992).

Bibliography

A. Powell (editor), *Euripides, Women and Sexuality* (London: Routledge, 1990).

D. Pralon, *Les travaux d'Héraclès dans L'Héraclès Furieux d'Euripide*. (*Héraclès Furieux vv. 348-441*), in Moreau, *L'initiation II*, pp. 5-17.

S. Price & E. Kearns (editors), *The Oxford Dictionary of Classical Myth and Religion* (Oxford: Oxford University Press, 2003).

S.L. Radt, C.J. Ruijgh (editors), *Miscellanea Tragica in Honorem J.C. Kamerbeek* (Amsterdam: Hakkert, 1976).

G. Raepsaet, 'Les motivations de la natalité à Athènes aux Ve et IVe siècles avant notre ère', *Antiquité Classique* 40 (1971), pp. 80-110.

B. Rawson, 'Pompey and Hercules', *Antichthon* 4 (1970), pp. 30-7.

R. Rehm, 'Performing the Chorus. Choral Action, Interaction and Absence in Euripides', *Arion* 3rd series, 4.1 (1996), pp. 45-60.

——— 'Before, Behind, Beyond: Tragic Space and Euripides' *Heracles*', in Cropp & Lee, *Euripides and Tragic Theatre*, pp. 363-75.

——— *The Play of Space* (Princeton: Princeton University Press, 2002).

K. Riley, 'Heracles as Dr Strangelove and GI Joe: Male Heroism Deconstructed', in Hall, Macintosh & Wrigley, *Dionysus Since 69: Greek Tragedy at the Dawn of the Third Millennium*, pp. 113-42.

W. Ritchie, *The Authenticity of the Rhesus of Euripides* (Cambridge: Cambridge University Press, 1964).

S. Ritter, *Hercules in der römischen Kunst von den Anfängen bis Augustus* (Heidelberg: Archäologie und Geschichte 5, 1995).

A. Rivier, *Essai sur le tragique d'Euripide* (Paris: Les Belles Lettres, 1975).

K. Robb, *Literacy and Paideia in Ancient Greece* (Oxford: Oxford University Press, 1994).

E. Robbins, 'The Education of Achilles', *Quaderni urbinati di cultura classica* 45 (1993), pp. 7-22.

D.H. Roberts, 'Outside the Drama: The Limits of Tragedy in Aristotle's *Poetics*', in Rorty, *Essays on Aristotle's Poetics*, pp. 13-153.

D.H. Roberts, F.M. Dunn & D. Fowler (editors), *Classical Closure. Reading the End in Greek and Latin Literature* (Princeton: Princeton University Press, 1997).

N. Robertson, 'Heracles' Catabasis', *Hermes* 108 (1980), pp. 274-300.

B. Rochette, 'Héraclès à la croissé des chemins', *Les Études Classiques* 66 (1998), pp. 105-13.

V. Rodgers, 'Some Thoughts on Dike', *Classical Quarterly n.s.* 21 (1971), pp. 289-301.

J. de Romilly, 'Le refus du suicide dans l'Héraclès d'Euripide', *Archaeognosia* 1 (1980), pp. 1-10.

A.O. Rorty (editor), *Essays on Aristotle's Poetics* (Princeton: Princeton University Press, 1992).

Bibliography

K. Rosen (editor), *Macht und Kultur im Rom der Kaiserzeit* (Bonn: Bouvier, 1994).

L. Rubinstein, *Adoption in IVth Century Athens* (Copenhagen: Museum Tusculanum Press, 1993).

C.A.P. Ruck, 'Duality and the Madness of Herakles', *Arethusa* 9 (1976), pp. 53-76.

B.S. Sangharakshita, *Hercules and the Birds* (London: Windhorse Press, 1996).

M. Schmidt, 'Medea und Herakles. Zwei tragische Kindermörder', in Böhr & Martini, *Studien zur Mythologie und Vasenmalerei*, pp. 169-74.

A. Schnapp-Gourbeillon, *Lions, héros, masques. Les représentations de l'animal chéz Homère* (Paris: Maspero, 1981).

R. Seaford, *Ritual and Reciprocity. Homer and Tragedy in the Developing City State* (Oxford: Clarendon Press, 1994).

D. Seale, *Vision and Stagecraft in Sophocles* (Chicago: University of Chicago Press, 1982).

E. Segal, *Euripides and the Poetics of Sorrow. Art, Gender and Commemoration in Alcestis, Hippolytus, and Hecuba* (Durham & London: Duke University Press, 1993).

B. Seidensticker, 'Women on the Tragic Stage', in Goff, *History, Tragedy, Theory*, pp. 151-73.

J. Seznec, *La survivance des dieux antiques* (London: Studies of the Warburg Institute, vol. IX, 1940).

P. Sfyroeras, 'The Ironies of Salvation. The Aigeus Scene in Euripides' *Medea*', *Classical Journal* 90 (1994), pp. 125-42.

M.C. Shamun, 'Significaciones de taragma (perturbacíon) en Heracles de Euripides', *Synthesis* 4 (1997), pp. 99-112.

H.A. Shapiro, *Personifications in Greek Art* (Zurich: Akanthus, 1993).

J. Shay, *Achilles in Vietnam: Combat Trauma and the Undoing of Character* (New York: Atheneum, 1994).

J.A. Shelton, *Seneca's Hercules Furens: Theme, Structure and Style* (Hypomnemata S.) (Göttingen: Vandenhoeck and Ruprecht, 1978).

—— 'Structural Unity and the Meaning of Euripides' *Herakles*', *Eranos* 77 (1979), pp. 101-10.

F.L. Shisler, 'The Use of Stage Business to Portray Emotion in Greek Tragedy', *American Journal of Philology* 46 (1945), pp. 377-97.

P. Siewert, 'The Ephebic Oath in Fifth Century Athens', *Journal of Hellenic Studies* 97 (1997), pp. 102-11.

M.S. Silk, 'Heracles and Greek Tragedy', *Greece and Rome* 32 (1985), pp. 1-22.

—— (editor), *Tragedy and the Tragic. Greek Theatre and Beyond* (Oxford: Clarendon Press, 1996).

—— *Aristophanes and the Definition of Comedy*, (Oxford: Oxford University Press, 2000).

B. Simon, *Mind and Madness in Ancient Greece* (Ithaca: Cornell University Press, 1978).

—— *Tragic Drama and the Family* (New Haven: Yale University Press, 1988).

P.E. Slater, *The Glory of Hera* (Boston: Beacon, 1986).

R.R.R. Smith, *Hellenistic Sculpture* (London: Thames and Hudson, 1991).

A.H. Sommerstein, *Aeschylean Tragedy* (Bari: Levante, 1996).

—— *Greek Drama and Dramatists* (London: Routledge, 2002).

A.H. Sommerstein, S. Halliwell, J. Henderson & B. Zimmerman (editors), *Tragedy, Comedy and the Polis* (Bari: Levante, 1993).

S.E. Sorum, 'Monsters and the Family: The Exodus of Sophocles' Trachiniae', *Greek, Roman and Byzantine Studies* 19 (1978), pp. 59-74.

C. Sourvinou-Inwood, *Theseus as Son and Stepson*: *A Tentative Illustration of the Greek Mythological Mentality* (London: Institute of Classical Studies, 1979).

—— 'Reading' *Greek Culture* (Oxford: Clarendon Press, 1991).

—— 'Reading' *Greek Death* (Oxford: Clarendon Press, 1995).

—— 'Something to do with Athens: Tragedy and Ritual', in Osborne & Hornblower, *Ritual, Finance, Politics*, pp. 269-89.

—— 'Images and Euripidean Tragedy', in Clauss & Johnston, *Medea*, pp. 156-78.

E. Stafford, *Worshipping Virtues*: *Personification and the Divine in Ancient Greece* (Cardiff: Classical Press of Wales, 2001).

D.T. Steiner, 'Stoning and Sight – a Structural Equivalence in Greek Myth', *Classical Antiquity* 14 (1995), pp. 193-211.

P.T. Stevens, *Colloquial Expressions in Euripides* (Wiesbaden: Franz Steiner Verlag GMBH. Hermes Heft 38, 1976).

D.L. Stockton, *The Classical Athenian Democracy* (Oxford: Clarendon Press, 1990).

I.C. Storey & A. Allen, *A Guide to Ancient Greek Drama* (Oxford: Blackwell, 2005).

B.S. Strauss, *Fathers and Sons in Athens*: *Ideology and Society in the Era of the Peloponnesian War* (Princeton: Princeton University Press, 1993).

C. Stray, *Classics Transformed*: *Schools, Universities and Society in England 1830-1960* (Oxford: Clarendon Press, 1998).

D.F. Sutton, 'The Relation Between Tragedies and Fourth Place Plays in Three Instances', *Arethusa* 4 (1971), pp. 55-72.

—— *The Greek Satyr Play* (Meisenheim: Anton Hain, 1980).

O. Taplin, *The Stagecraft of Aeschylus*: *The Dramatic Uses of Exits and Entrances in Greek Tragedy* (Oxford: Clarendon Press, 1977a).

—— 'Did Greek Dramatists Write Stage Instructions?', *Proceedings of the Cambridge Philological Society* 23 (1977b), pp. 121-32.

—— *Greek Tragedy in Action* (London: Methuen, 1983).

—— (1995), 'Opening Performance. Closing Texts', *Essays in Criticism* 45.2 (1995), pp. 93-104.

—— 'Comedy and the Tragic', in Silk, *Tragedy and the Tragic*, pp. 188-203.

—— 'The Pictorial Record', in Easterling, *The Cambridge Companion to Greek Tragedy*, pp. 69-92.

T.A. Tarkow, 'The Glorification of Athens in Euripides' *Heracles*', *Helios* 5 (1977), pp. 27-35.

—— 'Thematic Implications of Costuming in the *Oresteia*', *Maia* 32 (1980), pp. 153-66.

S.C. Todd, *The Shape of Athenian Law* (Oxford: Clarendon Press, 1993).

R. Turcan, *The Gods of Ancient Rome*, translated by A. Nevill (Edinburgh: Edinburgh University Press, 2000).

A. Turyn, *Byzantine Manuscript Tradition of the Tragedies of Euripides* (Urbana: University of Illinois Press, 1957).

J.P. Uhlenbrock, *Herakles: Passage of a Hero Through 1000 Years of Classical Art* (New Rochelle, NY; Annandale-on-Hudson, NY: A.D. Caratzas: Edith C. Blum Art Institute, Bard College, 1986).

R.G. Ussher, *Sophocles: Philoctetes* (Warminster: Aris & Phillips, 1990).

A. Verbanck-Piérard, 'Le double culte d'Héraklès: légende ou réalité?', in Laurens, *Entre hommes et dieux. Le convive, le héros, le prophète*, pp. 43-65.

W.J. Verdenius, 'Notes on Euripides' Herakles vv. 1-522', *Mnemosyne* 15 (1987), pp. 1-17.

J.-P. Vernant, 'At Man's Table: Hesiod's Foundation Myth of Sacrifice', in Detienne & Vernant, *The Cuisine of Sacrifice among the Greeks*, pp. 40-63.

J.-P. Vernant & J. Vidal-Naquet, *Myth and Tragedy in Ancient Greece* (New York: Oxford University Press, translated by J. Lloyd, 1990).

M. Vickers, 'Heracles Lacedaemonius: The Political Dimension of Sophocles' *Trachiniae* and Euripides' *Heracles*', *Dialogues d'Histoire Ancienne* 21.2 (1995), pp. 41-69.

S. Vilatte, 'La nourrice greque: une question d'histoire sociale et religieuse', *L'Antiquité Classique* 60 (1991), pp. 5-28.

R. Volkommer, *Herakles in the Art of Classical Greece* (Oxford, Oxford University Committee for Archaeology Monograph No. 25, 1988).

H. Walker, *Theseus and Athens* (New York & Oxford: Oxford University Press, 1995).

J.M. Walton, *Greek Theatre Practice* (Westport Conn: Greenwood Press, 1980).

P. Wathelet, 'Rhésos ou la quête de l'immortalité', *Kernos* 3 (1989), pp. 213-32.

—— 'Les enfances extraordinaires dans la mythologie grecque', *Les Études Classiques* 64 (1993), pp. 109-26.

P.A. Watson, *Ancient Stepmothers: Myth, Misogyny and Reality* (Leiden; Brill, 1995).

M.L. West, *Greek Metre* (Oxford: Clarendon Press, 1982).

—— *Ancient Greek Music* (Oxford: Clarendon, 1992).

U. Von Wilamowitz-Moellendorff, *Euripides: Herakles*, 3 vols (Darmstadt: Wissenschaftliche Buchgesellschaft, 1959, 3 vols (Berlin: 1895)).

J. Wilkins, 'The State and the Individual: Euripides' Plays of Voluntary Self-Sacrifice', in Powell, *Euripides, Women and Sexuality*, pp. 177-94.

R. Winken, 'Hercules in the Art of the Republic', *Journal of Roman Archaeology* 9 (1996), pp. 328-41.

J.J. Winkler 'The Ephebes' Song: *Tragoidia* and *Polis*', in Winkler & Zeitlin, *Nothing To Do With Dionysos?*, pp. 20-64.

J.J. Winkler & F.I. Zeitlin (editors), *Nothing To Do With Dionysos? Athenian Drama in its Social Context* (Princeton: Princeton University Press, 1990).

S. Woodford, 'The Cults of Herakles in Attica', in Mitten, Pedley & Scott, *Studies Presented to George M.A. Hanfmann*, pp. 211-26.

N. Worman, 'The Ties That Bind: Transformations of Costume and Connection in Euripides' *Heracles*', *Ramus* 28 (1999), pp. 89-107.

S. Yoshitake, 'Disgrace, Grief and Other Ills: Heracles' Rejection of Suicide', *Journal of Hellenic Studies* 114 (1994), pp. 135-53.

H. Yunis, 'A New Creed: Heracles', in H. Yunis, *A New Creed. Fundamental Beliefs in the Athenian Polis and Euripidean Drama* (Göttingen: *Hypomnemata* 91,1998), pp. 139-71.

F.I. Zeitlin, 'The Motif of the Corrupted Sacrifice in Aeschylus' *Oresteia*', *Transactions of the American Philology Association* 96 (1965), pp. 463-508.

G. Zuntz, *An Inquiry into the Transmission of the Plays of Euripides* (Cambridge: Cambridge University Press, 1965).

Glossary

Aetion (pl. ***aetia***). The reason given for the existence of ritual practices.

Aetiology. Literally 'an explanation' (from the Greek *aition*, cause). The term is used in discussion of mythology to indicate a myth which purports to explain the origins and rationale of social or ritual practices.

City Dionysia. Annual festival for the god Dionysus held in Athens. Also referred to as the 'Great Dionysia'.

Didaskalos. The playwright/director.

Ekkyklêma. Trolley, a wheeled platform used to bring interior scenes outside.

Hybris. An act of arrogance towards the gods.

Katabasis. Literally 'a descent', used in discussions of religion and mythology to describe a descent into Hades.

Kurios. The legal head of an *oikos*, the adult male who had control over children and women in the household.

Liminal. Referring to something on a boundary or in transition between two states.

Mêchanê. The crane which could bring flying characters, particularly gods, into the theatre.

Metatheatre. A style of drama which plays with its own dramatic illusion, inviting the audience to contemplate the nature of art and reality.

Nemesis. Divine punishment for committing an act of *hybris*.

Oikos. Household/family.

Orchêstra. Literally 'dancing space'. The flat area between the audience and the actors where the chorus performed. In later fourth-century theatres the space was semi-circular.

Parodos. The opening song from a chorus in tragedy, usually delivered as the chorus members entered the theatre and sung in a marching rhythm.

Philia. Love or affection, particulary for friends or family, as opposed to *eros*, romantic, sexual love.

Polis. City-state.

Protagonist. The principal actor.

Satyr play. Comic performance staged after a series of three tragedies.

Sophist. A professional teacher of philosophy and public speaking.

Stichomythia. Dialogue in which each speaker only delivers one line of verse at a time.

Tropheia. Nurture, in particular the mutual obligations between parent and child.

Chronology

All dates are BCE unless otherwise indicated.

c. 8th/7th cent: Composition of the Homeric epics, *Iliad* and *Odyssey*.

c. 533: The City Dionysia festival established in Athens.

501: First official records made of contests in the City Dionysia.

490: First Persian invasion, Persians defeated at the Battle of Marathon.

481-479: Second Persian invasion of Greece.

c. 480: Birth of Euripides.

c. 456: Death of Aeschylus.

455: Euripides competes in his first competition, and comes last. No plays surviving from these productions.

431: Start of the Peloponnesian War between Athens and the Peloponnesians led by Sparta.

431: Euripides' *Medea* produced as a part of a trilogy which comes last.

?425-16: First production of *Heracles*.

415: Launch of Athenian expedition against Sicily (defeated in 413).

406/7: Death of Euripides. Two plays produced posthumously survive, *Bacchae* and *Iphigeneia in Aulis*.

405: Production of Aristophanes' *Frogs*.

384-322: Life of the philosopher Aristotle.

356-323: Life of Alexander 'The Great'.

?270-45: Composition of Apollonius Rhodius' epic poem *Argonautica*.

70-19: Life of Virgil, author of the *Aeneid*.

31: Battle of Actium; control of Roman world passes to Octavian, later known as the Emperor Augustus.

? c. 52 CE: Composition of Seneca's play *Hercules Furens*.

54-68 CE: Reign of the Emperor Nero.

180-192 CE: Reign of the Emperor Commodus.

Index

Index

174